Graph-Powered LLMs

How Graph Retrieval is Revolutionizing Large Language Model Capabilities

Sergio Robert

Table of Contents

Preface

Hey there! Ever felt like those amazing language AI things, the ones writing poems and stories, are missing something? Like, they can write like Shakespeare, but sometimes flub basic facts or get confused easily? You're not alone! That's what got me, and a lot of other AI folks, thinking: how do we give these Large Language Models (LLMs) a real boost of smarts?

Background and Motivation

Think of it like this: LLMs are great at language, but they don't truly *understand* the world. They need a knowledge base, a way to connect facts and ideas like we do. That's where knowledge graphs come in. Imagine a web of information, where everything is linked in a meaningful way. By connecting LLMs to these graphs, we can give them access to a whole universe of facts, relationships, and context. That's the magic of Graph Retrieval-Augmented Generation, or Graph RAG for short!

Purpose and Scope

This book, "Graph-Powered LLMs: How Graph Retrieval is Revolutionizing Large Language Model Capabilities," is your guide to this exciting new frontier in AI. We'll break down the what, why, and how of Graph RAG, exploring how it's making LLMs more accurate, insightful, and downright impressive.

Target Audience

Whether you're an AI researcher pushing the boundaries of knowledge, a developer building the next generation of AI applications, or just someone with a curious mind wanting to understand the future of language AI, this book is for you. We'll keep things clear and engaging, with plenty of real-world examples to show how Graph RAG is already making a difference.

Organization and Structure

We'll start with the basics, laying the groundwork for understanding LLMs and knowledge graphs. Then, we'll explore the core techniques of graph retrieval and see how they supercharge LLM abilities. From there, we'll explore the amazing applications of Graph RAG, from chatbots that actually get you to knowledge-powered search engines that go beyond simple keywords. We'll even peek under the hood of some real-world projects and discuss the challenges and opportunities that lie ahead.

Invitation to Read

So, buckle up and get ready to explore the fascinating world of graph-powered LLMs! This book is your invitation to understand how this technology is shaping the future of AI and, ultimately, how we interact with information and each other. Let's unlock the true potential of LLMs together!

Chapter 1: The Limitations of Current LLMs

Alright, let's get this show on the road! We're about to step into the fascinating world of Large Language Models (LLMs), those incredible AI systems that can write stories, translate languages, and answer your questions in a way that seems almost... human. But before we dive headfirst into how we can make these LLMs even more awesome with graph retrieval, let's take a moment to understand where they currently shine and where they, well, maybe need a little extra help.

1.1 The Promise and Challenges of LLMs

LLMs are truly revolutionizing how we interact with computers and information. They've opened up a whole new world of possibilities, allowing us to:

- Generate human-quality text: LLMs can write stories, poems, articles, and even code with remarkable fluency and creativity.[1] They can adapt their writing style to mimic different authors or genres, making them incredibly versatile tools for content creation.[2]
- Translate languages: Gone are the days of clunky, literal translations. LLMs can translate languages with impressive accuracy and nuance, capturing the subtleties and idioms that make each language unique.[3] This has huge implications for communication and understanding across cultures.
- Answer questions and summarize information: Need to quickly grasp the main points of a lengthy document? LLMs can provide concise and informative summaries, saving you time and effort.[4] They can also answer your questions in a comprehensive and informative way, even if they're open-ended, challenging, or strange.[5]

- Engage in conversations: LLMs are powering a new generation of chatbots and conversational agents that can engage in more natural and meaningful interactions.[6] They can understand your intent, remember previous turns in the conversation, and respond in ways that are both informative and engaging.[7]
- Personalize experiences: LLMs can be used to personalize everything from product recommendations to educational content.[8] By understanding your preferences and needs, they can tailor information and experiences to make them more relevant and helpful.

These are just a few examples of the incredible potential that LLMs hold. As they continue to evolve, we can expect even more groundbreaking applications in fields like healthcare, education, customer service, and scientific research.

1.2 The Challenges of LLMs

Alright, let's get real for a moment. While Large Language Models (LLMs) have made incredible strides and offer a glimpse into the future of AI, they're not without their shortcomings. In fact, understanding these limitations is crucial if we want to build truly robust and trustworthy AI systems. So, let's take off the rose-tinted glasses and have an honest conversation about the challenges that LLMs still face.

1. Factual Accuracy and Hallucinations

One of the biggest hurdles for LLMs is their tendency to generate incorrect or misleading information, even if it sounds perfectly plausible. It's like they're excellent storytellers who sometimes get carried away with their own narratives, blurring the lines between fact and fiction.

This phenomenon, often referred to as "hallucination," can have serious consequences. Imagine an LLM being used in a medical setting, confidently recommending a treatment based on a research paper that doesn't actually exist. Or consider a legal scenario where an LLM misinterprets case law, potentially leading to flawed legal arguments.

Why does this happen? Well, LLMs are trained on massive amounts of text data, but this data can be messy, containing errors, biases, and outdated information. The models learn to mimic patterns in the data, but they don't have a built-in fact-checking mechanism or a way to verify the reliability of their sources.

Here's a simplified example

Let's say we train an LLM on a dataset with these two sentences:

- "The Earth is flat."
- "The Earth is a sphere."

The LLM might learn that both statements are equally valid because they both appear in the data. It might then generate a sentence like:

- "Some people believe the Earth is flat, while others believe it is a sphere, and both perspectives are equally correct."

This is obviously wrong, but the LLM has no way of knowing that. It simply reflects the patterns it has observed in the data.

2. Common Sense Reasoning

As humans, we rely on a vast amount of common sense knowledge to navigate the world. We know that objects fall when dropped, that walls can't be walked through, and that cats can't breathe underwater. But LLMs often struggle with these basic concepts.

Why? Because common sense isn't explicitly written down in most of the text they learn from. It's something we acquire through lived experience, interacting with the physical world and observing how things work. LLMs, on the other hand, primarily learn from text, which can be abstract and lack the grounding in physical reality that we have.

This lack of common sense can lead to some amusing, and sometimes concerning, outputs. An LLM might generate a story where someone drives a car through a lake or a recipe that calls for boiling ice cubes. These errors might seem humorous, but they highlight a fundamental challenge in AI: how do we teach machines to understand the world in the same way we do?

3. Contextual Understanding and Memory

Another hurdle for LLMs is maintaining a consistent understanding of context over longer stretches of text or conversation. They can process information in a sentence or paragraph, but they often struggle to remember and integrate information from earlier parts of the interaction.

Think of it like having a conversation with someone who has a very short attention span. They might respond appropriately to your last sentence but completely forget what you were talking about five minutes ago. This can lead to confusing and frustrating interactions.

This limitation stems from the way LLMs process information. They typically use a "sliding window" approach, focusing on a limited chunk of text at a time. This allows them to generate fluent and coherent responses in the short term, but it makes it difficult for them to maintain a long-term memory of the conversation or document.

4. Bias and Fairness

LLMs are trained on massive datasets of text and code scraped from the internet, books, and other sources. These datasets can reflect and amplify societal biases, leading to LLMs generating outputs that are discriminatory, offensive, or harmful.

For example, an LLM trained on news articles might associate certain professions with specific genders or ethnicities, leading it to generate biased statements like "The surgeon was a man" or "The nurse was a woman." These biases can perpetuate harmful stereotypes and reinforce existing inequalities.

Addressing bias in LLMs is a complex and ongoing challenge. It requires careful consideration of the training data, the model architecture, and the evaluation metrics used to assess the model's performance.

5. Explainability and Interpretability

LLMs are often described as "black boxes" because it can be difficult to understand why they generate a particular output. This lack of transparency can make it challenging to trust LLMs or to debug them when they make mistakes.

Imagine an LLM being used to make loan approval decisions. If the model rejects an application, it's important to understand *why* it made that decision. Was it based on relevant factors like credit score and income, or was it influenced by biases in the training data?

Researchers are developing techniques to make LLMs more explainable and interpretable, but this remains an active area of research.

6. Computational Cost

Training and deploying LLMs can be computationally expensive, requiring specialized hardware and significant energy consumption. This can limit their accessibility and create environmental concerns.

Researchers are exploring ways to make LLMs more efficient, such as developing new model architectures and training methods that require less computational power.

Moving Forward

These challenges highlight the importance of ongoing research and development in the field of LLMs. As we continue to push the boundaries of what these models can do, we must also be mindful of their limitations and work towards creating AI systems that are safe, reliable, and beneficial for everyone.

I hope this frank discussion about the challenges of LLMs has been helpful. It's crucial to understand these limitations so we can develop and use these powerful tools responsibly. In the next chapter, we'll explore how knowledge graphs can help address some of these challenges and unlock the full potential of LLMs.

1.3 Addressing the Challenges

Now that we've had an honest conversation about the limitations of LLMs, you might be wondering, "So, what can we do about it?" Don't worry, it's not all doom and gloom! The good news is that researchers and developers around the world are actively working on solutions to these challenges.[1]

Let's explore some of the exciting approaches they're taking:

1. Improving Training Data: It All Starts at the Source

Think of it like this: if you feed an LLM a diet of junk food (inaccurate, biased, or outdated information), it's not going to produce healthy outputs. That's why improving the quality of training data is crucial.

Here are some ways researchers are tackling this

- Curating high-quality datasets: Instead of just scraping massive amounts of data from the internet, researchers are focusing on creating more carefully curated datasets.[2] This involves selecting sources known for their accuracy and reliability, and filtering out noisy or biased information.
- Adding more diverse data: To reduce bias, it's essential to ensure that training data represents a wide range of perspectives and experiences.[3] This means including data from different cultures, languages, and demographics.
- Fact-checking and validation: Researchers are developing techniques to automatically fact-check the information in training data, identifying and correcting errors before they're fed to the LLM.

2. Incorporating Knowledge Graphs: Giving LLMs a World Model

Remember how we talked about LLMs lacking common sense and struggling with context? Well, knowledge graphs can help with that!

A knowledge graph is like a map of the world, representing entities (people, places, things) and the relationships between them.[4] By connecting LLMs to knowledge graphs, we can give them access to a structured knowledge base, allowing them to:

- Reason more effectively: With a knowledge graph, an LLM can understand that a "bird" is a type of "animal" and that "animals" need "oxygen" to breathe.[5] This allows it to make more logical inferences and avoid generating nonsensical statements.
- Understand context: Knowledge graphs can provide valuable context for LLMs. For example, if an LLM encounters the sentence "The president gave a speech," it can use a knowledge graph to identify which president is

being referred to and what the context of the speech might be.

- Generate more accurate responses: By grounding their responses in a knowledge graph, LLMs can provide more accurate and reliable information.[6]

3. Developing New Architectures: Rethinking the LLM Brain

The architecture of an LLM refers to its underlying structure and how it processes information.[7] Researchers are constantly exploring new architectures to improve LLM capabilities and address their limitations.[8]

Here are some examples

- Transformer networks with memory: These architectures incorporate memory mechanisms that allow LLMs to retain information over longer periods, improving their ability to handle context and maintain coherence.[9]
- Neuro-symbolic AI: This approach combines the strengths of neural networks (like LLMs) with symbolic AI, which uses logical rules and symbols to represent knowledge.[10] This can improve LLMs' ability to reason and explain their decisions.
- Modular architectures: These architectures break down LLMs into smaller, more specialized modules that can be trained and updated independently.[11] This can make LLMs more efficient and adaptable.

4. Reinforcement Learning from Human Feedback: Training with a Teacher

Imagine having a teacher who constantly provides feedback and guidance as you learn. That's the idea behind reinforcement learning from human feedback (RLHF).

In RLHF, humans provide feedback on the quality of LLM outputs, rewarding good responses and penalizing bad ones.[12] This feedback is used to fine-tune the LLM, improving its ability to generate relevant, accurate, and appropriate responses.[13]

This approach is particularly useful for addressing issues like bias and toxicity. By training LLMs with human feedback, we can encourage them to generate outputs that are aligned with human values and preferences.

5. Improving Explainability and Interpretability: Opening the Black Box

As we discussed earlier, one of the challenges with LLMs is their lack of transparency. It can be difficult to understand why an LLM generates a particular output, which can make it challenging to trust or debug them.

Researchers are developing techniques to make LLMs more explainable and interpretable.[14] This includes

- Attention mechanisms: These mechanisms highlight the parts of the input text that the LLM is focusing on when generating its output, providing insights into its decision-making process.[15]
- Probing techniques: These techniques involve testing LLMs with specific prompts or questions to understand their internal representations and how they process information.[16]
- Rule extraction: This involves extracting logical rules from LLMs, making their decision-making process more transparent.[17]

6. Addressing Computational Cost: Making LLMs More Efficient

Training and deploying LLMs can be computationally expensive, requiring specialized hardware and significant energy consumption.[18] This can limit their accessibility and raise environmental concerns.

To address this, researchers are exploring

- Model compression: This involves reducing the size of LLMs without significantly sacrificing their performance.[19]
- Efficient training methods: Researchers are developing new training methods that require less computational power and energy.[20]
- Specialized hardware: Companies are developing specialized hardware designed specifically for running LLMs, making them more efficient and accessible.[21]

The Road Ahead

Addressing the challenges of LLMs is an ongoing process, but the progress we're making is truly exciting. By combining these different approaches, we can create LLMs that are more accurate, reliable, and beneficial for everyone.

As we continue this journey, it's important to remember that LLMs are powerful tools that can be used for good or for ill. It's up to us to ensure that they're developed and used responsibly, with a focus on fairness, transparency, and human well-being.

I hope this discussion has given you a sense of the exciting developments happening in the field of LLMs. It's a rapidly evolving area, and I'm eager to see what the future holds! Now, let's move on to the next chapter and explore how knowledge graphs can help us unlock the full potential of these amazing models.

1.4 Common Sense Reasoning and Knowledge Gaps

You know, it's funny how we humans take common sense for granted. We effortlessly navigate the world, understanding that birds fly, water is wet, and you can't walk through walls. But for LLMs, these seemingly simple concepts can be surprisingly challenging. It's like they're brilliant students who aced all their exams but somehow missed out on basic life skills.

This lack of common sense reasoning is a major hurdle for LLMs, preventing them from truly understanding the world and generating outputs that are consistently grounded in reality. Let's explore why this happens and what we can do about it.

Why LLMs Struggle with Common Sense

Think about how you learned common sense. It wasn't through reading textbooks or memorizing facts. It was through experiencing the world firsthand, interacting with objects, and observing how things work. You learned that hot stoves burn by (hopefully not!) touching one, and you learned that gravity pulls things down by dropping toys as a baby.

LLMs, on the other hand, primarily learn from text. They devour massive amounts of written information, but they don't have the same kind of physical embodiment and real-world interaction that we do. This means they miss out on the rich, sensory experiences that shape our understanding of the world.

As a result, LLMs can sometimes generate outputs that defy common sense. They might write a story where someone drives a car through a lake or a recipe that calls for boiling ice cubes. These errors might seem humorous, but they highlight a fundamental challenge in AI: how do we teach machines to understand the world in the same way we do?

The Knowledge Gap

Beyond common sense, LLMs can also suffer from knowledge gaps. They might be able to discuss complex scientific theories or historical events, but struggle to answer simple questions about everyday life. This is because their knowledge is limited to the data they were trained on, which may not cover the full breadth of human experience.

For example, an LLM might be able to explain the theory of relativity but be unable to tell you how to make a cup of tea. Or it might be able to generate a detailed analysis of Shakespeare's plays but struggle to understand the rules of a simple card game.

These knowledge gaps can limit the ability of LLMs to engage in meaningful conversations, generate relevant responses, and perform tasks that require real-world understanding.

Bridging the Gap

So, how can we help LLMs develop common sense and fill in their knowledge gaps?

Here are some approaches researchers are exploring:

- Incorporating Multimodal Data: Instead of relying solely on text, researchers are training LLMs on multimodal data, which includes images, videos, and sensory information. This can help LLMs develop a more grounded understanding of the world and learn common sense concepts through observation, just like humans do.
- Simulating Physical Interactions: Researchers are creating virtual environments where LLMs can interact with objects and learn about physics, cause and effect, and other common sense concepts. This allows them to gain experience and build a more intuitive understanding of how the world works.
- Leveraging Knowledge Graphs: As we discussed earlier, knowledge graphs can provide LLMs with a structured knowledge base, helping them fill in knowledge gaps and make more informed decisions. By connecting LLMs to knowledge graphs, we can give them access to a wealth of information about the world, from everyday objects and

concepts to complex scientific theories and historical events.

- Reinforcement Learning from Human Feedback: Training LLMs with reinforcement learning, using human feedback to guide their learning process, can help them develop common sense and learn to avoid generating nonsensical outputs. By rewarding LLMs for generating responses that are consistent with human understanding and penalizing them for generating nonsensical or illogical outputs, we can encourage them to develop a more grounded and realistic view of the world.

The Importance of Common Sense

Developing common sense reasoning and filling knowledge gaps is crucial for creating LLMs that are truly intelligent and capable of understanding and interacting with the world in a meaningful way. As we continue to push the boundaries of LLM capabilities, it's essential to remember that common sense and real-world knowledge are just as important as language skills.

By combining these different approaches, we can help LLMs bridge the gap between artificial intelligence and human understanding, creating AI systems that are not only intelligent but also grounded, reliable, and trustworthy.

I hope this discussion has shed some light on the challenges of common sense reasoning and knowledge gaps in LLMs. It's a fascinating area of research, and I'm excited to see how these challenges will be addressed in the years to come. Now, let's move on to the next challenge and explore how we can tackle the issue of bias and fairness in LLMs.

1.5 Contextual Understanding and Memory

Have you ever had a conversation with someone who seems to forget what you were talking about just a few sentences ago? It can be frustrating, right? Well, LLMs can sometimes face a similar challenge. While they can generate text that seems relevant in the moment, they can struggle to maintain a consistent understanding of the broader context, especially in longer conversations or documents.[1]

This limitation in contextual understanding and memory is a significant hurdle for LLMs, hindering their ability to engage in truly meaningful and coherent interactions.[2] Let's explore why this happens and what we can do about it.

The Limits of Short-Term Memory

Think about how you process information during a conversation. You don't just focus on the last sentence spoken; you keep track of the entire conversation, remembering key details, and building a mental model of what's being discussed. This allows you to understand the flow of the conversation, respond appropriately, and make connections between different ideas.

LLMs, on the other hand, often rely on a "sliding window" approach to processing information.[3] They focus on a limited chunk of text at a time, typically the last few sentences or paragraphs. This allows them to generate fluent and coherent responses in the short term, but it makes it difficult for them to maintain a long-term memory of the entire conversation or document.

As a result, LLMs can sometimes

- Lose track of previously mentioned details: They might forget names, dates, or key events that were mentioned earlier in the conversation.
- Contradict themselves: They might make statements that conflict with what they said earlier, creating confusion and inconsistency.[4]
- Go off on tangents: They might lose sight of the main topic and start generating responses that seem irrelevant or unrelated to the conversation.

This limited memory and contextual understanding can make it challenging for LLMs to engage in complex reasoning, maintain coherence over extended interactions, and generate outputs that are truly contextually relevant.[5]

Why Context Matters

Context is crucial for understanding and generating meaningful language.[6] It's like the background scenery in a play; it provides the setting, the relationships between characters, and the overall meaning of the story. Without context, words can be ambiguous, confusing, or even meaningless.[7]

For example, consider the sentence "He picked up the bat." Without context, we don't know if "he" is a baseball player or a vigilante, and we don't know if "the bat" is a baseball bat or a nocturnal animal. Context helps us disambiguate the meaning and understand the situation.[8]

LLMs need to be able to understand and utilize context to

- Resolve ambiguity: Identify the intended meaning of words and phrases based on the surrounding context.
- Track entities and relationships: Keep track of who is who and how they are related to each other in a conversation or story.

- Maintain coherence: Generate responses that are consistent with the overall topic and flow of the conversation.[9]
- Engage in complex reasoning: Make inferences and draw conclusions based on the information provided in the context.[10]

Enhancing Contextual Understanding and Memory

So, how can we help LLMs improve their contextual understanding and memory?

Here are some approaches researchers are exploring:

- Transformer Networks with Memory: Researchers are developing new LLM architectures that incorporate memory mechanisms, allowing them to store and retrieve information from earlier parts of the conversation or document.[11] This can help LLMs maintain a longer-term memory and better understand the context of the current interaction.
- Attention Mechanisms: Attention mechanisms allow LLMs to focus on the most relevant parts of the input text when generating a response.[12] This can help them better understand the context and generate more relevant and coherent outputs.
- Graph Neural Networks: Graph neural networks can be used to represent and process contextual information in a structured way.[13] This can help LLMs understand the relationships between different entities and events in a conversation or document, improving their ability to track context and maintain coherence.
- Reinforcement Learning from Human Feedback: Training LLMs with reinforcement learning, using human feedback to reward contextually appropriate responses, can encourage them to develop a better understanding of context and generate more coherent outputs.[14]

The Importance of Context

Improving contextual understanding and memory is essential for creating LLMs that can truly understand and interact with the world in a meaningful way. By addressing this challenge, we can unlock the full potential of LLMs and create AI systems that are more engaging, informative, and helpful.

I hope this discussion has given you a deeper understanding of the challenges and opportunities related to contextual understanding and memory in LLMs. It's an exciting area of research, and I'm eager to see how these challenges will be addressed in the years to come. Now, let's move on to the next challenge and explore how we can make LLMs more transparent and trustworthy by improving their explainability and interpretability.

1.6 The Need for External Knowledge Sources

We've talked about how LLMs can sometimes stumble when it comes to factual accuracy, common sense reasoning, and maintaining context. It's like they have all the words but not always the full picture of what those words mean in the real world. So, how do we bridge that gap? How do we give LLMs the grounding they need to truly understand and interact with the world around us?

The answer lies in external knowledge sources. Think of it like this: LLMs are like bright students who have learned a lot from textbooks, but they also need to go out into the world and experience things firsthand to gain a deeper understanding. External knowledge sources provide that real-world connection, giving LLMs access to a wealth of information that can enhance their capabilities and address their limitations.[1]

Why External Knowledge is Essential

LLMs, by themselves, are limited by the data they were trained on.[2] This data, while vast, is often incomplete, biased, or outdated.[3] It's like trying to understand the world by only reading encyclopedias from the 1950s – you'd miss out on a lot of important information!

External knowledge sources can provide LLMs with

- Up-to-date information: Access to constantly updated databases and knowledge repositories ensures that LLMs have the latest information on current events, scientific discoveries, and other evolving domains.[4]
- Factual accuracy: By grounding their responses in reliable external knowledge sources, LLMs can reduce the risk of generating inaccurate or misleading information.[5]
- Common sense knowledge: External knowledge sources can provide LLMs with the common sense knowledge they often lack, helping them understand basic concepts about the world and avoid generating nonsensical outputs.[6]
- Contextual understanding: By linking information from different sources, external knowledge can help LLMs understand the context of a conversation or document, improving their ability to generate relevant and coherent responses.[7]

Types of External Knowledge Sources

There are various types of external knowledge sources that can be used to enhance LLMs, each with its own strengths and limitations:

- Knowledge Graphs: We've already discussed knowledge graphs, which are structured representations of information that capture entities and their relationships.[8] They provide a powerful way to organize and access knowledge, allowing LLMs to reason more effectively, understand context, and generate more accurate responses.[9]

- Databases: Databases store vast amounts of structured data, such as customer information, financial records, and scientific data.[10] LLMs can access this data to answer questions, generate reports, and perform other data-driven tasks.[11]

- APIs: APIs (Application Programming Interfaces) allow LLMs to access information and services from other applications and systems.[12] This can provide them with real-time data, such as weather forecasts, stock prices, and social media trends.[13]

- Text Corpora: While LLMs are already trained on large text corpora, they can benefit from accessing specialized text collections, such as scientific papers, legal documents, or historical archives. This can provide them with domain-specific knowledge and improve their ability to answer questions and generate text in specific areas.[14]

Integrating External Knowledge with LLMs

Integrating external knowledge with LLMs is a complex but crucial task. It requires developing techniques to:

- Retrieve relevant information: LLMs need to be able to efficiently retrieve the most relevant information from external knowledge sources, given a specific query or context.[15]

- Reason over knowledge: LLMs need to be able to reason over the retrieved knowledge, making inferences and drawing conclusions based on the information provided.

- Integrate knowledge with language: LLMs need to be able to seamlessly integrate the retrieved knowledge with their language generation capabilities, generating responses that are both informative and coherent.[16]

Researchers are developing various approaches to achieve this, including:

- Graph Neural Networks: Graph neural networks can be used to process and reason over knowledge graphs, allowing LLMs to access and utilize the information stored in these graphs.[17]
- Retrieval-Augmented Generation: This approach involves retrieving relevant information from external knowledge sources and using it to augment the LLM's input, providing it with additional context and knowledge.[18]
- Neuro-symbolic AI: This approach combines the strengths of neural networks (like LLMs) with symbolic AI, which uses logical rules and symbols to represent knowledge.[19] This can improve LLMs' ability to reason over external knowledge and generate more explainable outputs.

The Future of Knowledge-Enhanced LLMs

The integration of external knowledge sources is transforming the landscape of LLMs, paving the way for a new generation of AI systems that are more knowledgeable, context-aware, and capable.[20] As we continue to develop and refine these techniques, we can expect LLMs to play an even greater role in our lives, helping us access information, make decisions, and solve problems in ways we never thought possible.

I hope this discussion has highlighted the importance of external knowledge sources in unlocking the full potential of LLMs. It's an exciting area of research, and I'm eager to see how these developments will shape the future of AI. Now, let's move on to the next chapter and explore the fascinating world of knowledge graphs in more detail.

Chapter 2: Introduction to Knowledge Graphs

In the last chapter, we talked about how LLMs can sometimes feel a bit like they're living in a bubble, lacking real-world knowledge and common sense. Well, one of the most exciting ways to address this is by connecting them to knowledge graphs. Think of knowledge graphs as a kind of "cheat sheet" for LLMs, giving them access to a treasure trove of information about the world.

2.1 What are Knowledge Graphs?

Okay, let's talk about knowledge graphs. You might have heard the term thrown around, but what exactly *are* they? In the simplest terms, a knowledge graph is a way of organizing information that's inspired by how *we* think. It's not just a list of facts, but a web of interconnected ideas.

Think of it like this: you know that "Paris" is a "city" and it's located in "France". You also know "France" is a "country" in "Europe". That's not just separate bits of trivia, it's *connected* knowledge. A knowledge graph makes those connections explicit.

More Than Just a Database

Now, you might be thinking, "Isn't that what a database does?" And you'd be partly right. Databases are great at storing information in an organized way.[1] But knowledge graphs go a step further. They don't just store data, they represent *knowledge*. They capture the meaning and relationships between things, allowing for a deeper understanding.[2]

Key Components of a Knowledge Graph

Let's break down the key ingredients that make a knowledge graph tick:

- Nodes: These are the building blocks of the graph. Each node represents an entity – a person, place, thing, concept, or even an event.[3] So, "Nelson Mandela", "Nigeria", "democracy", and "the Nigerian Civil War" could all be nodes in a knowledge graph.[4]
- Edges: These are the connections between the nodes.[5] They represent the relationships between entities.[6] For example, an edge might connect "Nelson Mandela" and "South Africa" with the relationship "president of".
- Labels: These provide meaning to the edges.[7] They tell us what kind of relationship exists between two nodes. Some common labels include "is a", "has a", "located in", "works for", "created by", and so on.

Why are Knowledge Graphs Important?

Knowledge graphs are becoming increasingly important in the world of AI because they allow machines to:

- Understand the world more like humans do: We don't just memorize isolated facts; we understand how those facts relate to each other. Knowledge graphs enable machines to do the same, moving beyond simple information retrieval to a more nuanced understanding of the world.[8]
- Reason and make inferences: By understanding relationships between entities, machines can make inferences and draw conclusions.[9] For example, if a knowledge graph knows that "Lagos" is in "Nigeria" and "Nigeria" is in "Africa", it can infer that "Lagos" is in "Africa".[10]
- Provide more accurate and relevant information: When searching for information, knowledge graphs can help

machines go beyond keyword matching and provide more accurate and relevant results by considering the context and relationships between entities.[11]

- Explain their reasoning: Because knowledge graphs are structured and explicit, they can provide a basis for explaining how a machine arrived at a particular conclusion or answer. This is crucial for building trust and transparency in AI systems.

Real-World Examples

You're probably interacting with knowledge graphs more often than you realize! Here are a few examples:

- Google Search: When you search for something on Google, the knowledge graph helps provide those informative boxes with key facts and related entities.[12]
- Social Networks: Social media platforms use knowledge graphs to understand the connections between users, recommend friends, and target advertising.[13]
- E-commerce: Online retailers use knowledge graphs to recommend products, personalize shopping experiences, and manage their product catalogs.[14]
- Healthcare: Knowledge graphs are being used to analyze patient data, identify potential drug interactions, and support medical research.[15]

Knowledge Graphs and LLMs

As we move forward in this book, you'll see how knowledge graphs are becoming essential for enhancing the capabilities of LLMs. By connecting LLMs to these rich sources of structured knowledge, we can help them overcome limitations in common sense reasoning, factual accuracy, and contextual understanding.

This is just the beginning of our exploration of knowledge graphs. In the next section, we'll take a closer look at the different types of knowledge graphs and how they're built and maintained.

2.2 Structure of Knowledge Graphs

Think of it like learning the grammar of a language – once you understand the basic building blocks, you can start to appreciate how they combine to create complex meaning.

Nodes

In a knowledge graph, everything revolves around *nodes*. Each node represents a distinct entity.[1] And when I say "entity", I mean anything that can be identified and described:

- Real-world objects: People (like "Chinua Achebe"), places ("Lagos"), organizations ("Google"), or even physical things like a specific "laptop" or a famous "painting".[2]
- Concepts: Abstract ideas like "democracy", "justice", "love", or "artificial intelligence".[3]
- Events: Things that happen, like "the Nigerian Independence Day" or "the release of ChatGPT".[4]

Essentially, if you can name it, it can be a node!

Edges

Now, nodes on their own are just isolated pieces of information. The real power of a knowledge graph comes from the *edges* that connect them. Edges represent the relationships between entities.[5]

Think of it like a family tree. You have nodes for each person, and edges that say "parent of" or "child of" to show how they're related.

In a knowledge graph, these relationships can be incredibly diverse:

- "is a": This indicates a type-of relationship.[6] For example, "a mango is a fruit".
- "has a": This shows possession or attributes. "A car has an engine".
- "located in": "Abuja is located in Nigeria".[7]
- "works for": "This engineer works for Tesla".
- "created by": "Things Fall Apart was written by Chinua Achebe".[8]

And these are just a few examples! The possibilities are endless, allowing you to capture all sorts of complex relationships between entities.

Labels

Edges aren't just lines; they have meaning. That meaning is provided by labels. Labels are like verbs that describe the action or relationship between the nodes.[9]

For example, in the statement "Wole Soyinka won the Nobel Prize", you'd have

- Node 1: Wole Soyinka
- Edge: won
- Node 2: Nobel Prize[10]

The label "won" tells us the specific relationship between the two entities.

Putting it All Together

This structure of nodes, edges, and labels is what makes knowledge graphs so powerful. It allows us to represent knowledge in a way that is:

- Explicit: The relationships between entities are clearly defined.
- Machine-readable: Computers can easily process and understand the information in a knowledge graph.[11]
- Interconnected: The graph structure allows us to explore connections and discover new relationships between entities.[12]

Real-World Example

Let's say we're building a knowledge graph for Nigerian literature. We might have nodes for

- Authors: Chinua Achebe, Wole Soyinka, Chimamanda Ngozi Adichie, etc.
- Books: Things Fall Apart, Half of a Yellow Sun, Ake: The Years of Childhood, etc.[13]
- Characters: Okonkwo, Kambili, Ugwu, etc.
- Themes: Colonialism, identity, family, etc.
- Literary movements: Postcolonial literature, modernism, etc.

We could then use edges and labels to connect these nodes, showing relationships like

- "Chinua Achebe wrote Things Fall Apart"
- "Things Fall Apart explores the theme of colonialism"[14]
- "Okonkwo is a character in Things Fall Apart"[15]
- "Chimamanda Ngozi Adichie is part of the modern literary movement"[16]

This knowledge graph could then be used to answer questions like

- "Which books explore the theme of identity?"
- "Who are the main characters in Half of a Yellow Sun?"
- "Which authors are associated with postcolonial literature?"

Beyond Simple Connections

The beauty of knowledge graphs is that they can represent not just simple relationships, but also more complex ones. You can have multiple edges between nodes, representing different types of relationships.[17] You can also have properties attached to nodes and edges, providing additional information about them.[18]

For example, the node for "Things Fall Apart" could have properties like "publication year" (1958) and "genre" (fiction).[19] The edge connecting "Chinua Achebe" and "Things Fall Apart" could have a property like "date written" (1957-1958).

This richness and flexibility make knowledge graphs a powerful tool for representing and reasoning about complex information. And as you'll see in the coming chapters, they play a crucial role in enhancing the capabilities of LLMs and unlocking their full potential.

2.3 Types of Knowledge Graphs

Now that you have a good grasp of the basic structure of knowledge graphs, let's explore the different flavors they come in. Just like there are different types of maps – road maps, topographic maps, political maps – there are different types of knowledge graphs, each designed for specific purposes and containing different kinds of information.

1. Open Knowledge Graphs: The Wikipedia of Knowledge

Think of open knowledge graphs as the "Wikipedia" of the knowledge graph world. They aim to capture general knowledge about the world, covering a wide range of topics and domains.

They're publicly accessible, meaning anyone can use them, contribute to them, and build applications on top of them.

Some popular examples of open knowledge graphs include:

- Wikidata: This massive knowledge graph is collaboratively edited, just like Wikipedia. It contains information about a vast array of entities, from historical figures and geographical locations to scientific concepts and works of art. You can find it powering those informative boxes on Google Search results.
- DBpedia: This knowledge graph extracts information from Wikipedia and structures it in a machine-readable format. It's a great resource for general knowledge and is often used in research and education.
- YAGO: Yet Another Great Ontology (YAGO) is a knowledge graph that combines information from Wikipedia, WordNet (a lexical database), and GeoNames (a geographical database). It's known for its high accuracy and coverage.

These open knowledge graphs are incredibly valuable resources for LLMs. They provide a broad base of knowledge that can help LLMs understand the world, answer general knowledge questions, and generate more informed responses.

2. Domain-Specific Knowledge Graphs: Experts in Their Fields

While open knowledge graphs are great for general knowledge, sometimes you need something more specialized. That's where domain-specific knowledge graphs come in. These graphs focus on a particular area of knowledge, such as medicine, finance, law, or even a specific industry like agriculture or manufacturing.

For example, a medical knowledge graph might contain information about diseases, symptoms, treatments, drugs, and their interactions. A financial knowledge graph might include information about companies, stocks, markets, and economic indicators.

These specialized knowledge graphs are built with a specific purpose in mind and often use specialized vocabulary and ontologies (formal representations of knowledge) relevant to their domain. They're incredibly valuable for LLMs that need to operate within a specific field, allowing them to:

- Understand domain-specific language: LLMs can learn the terminology and jargon used in a particular field, enabling them to communicate more effectively with experts and understand specialized documents.
- Access relevant knowledge: Domain-specific knowledge graphs provide LLMs with direct access to the information they need for a particular task or application, without having to sift through irrelevant information.
- Reason and make inferences within the domain: LLMs can leverage the relationships and rules within a domain-specific knowledge graph to make inferences and draw conclusions relevant to that field.

3. Enterprise Knowledge Graphs: The Company's Brain

Imagine a company where all its knowledge – about its products, customers, processes, and employees – is organized and interconnected in a single, easily accessible system. That's the power of an enterprise knowledge graph.

These private knowledge graphs are used within organizations to:

- Improve decision-making: By providing a holistic view of the company's data and knowledge, enterprise knowledge graphs can support better-informed decisions.
- Enhance customer service: Enterprise knowledge graphs can be used to provide more personalized and relevant

customer service, by giving customer service agents quick access to customer information and relevant knowledge.

- Optimize operations: By capturing and analyzing data about business processes, enterprise knowledge graphs can help identify bottlenecks and inefficiencies, leading to improved operations.
- Drive innovation: By connecting different data sources and uncovering hidden relationships, enterprise knowledge graphs can spark new ideas and drive innovation.

For LLMs, enterprise knowledge graphs offer a way to tap into a company's internal knowledge and expertise, allowing them to:

- Answer questions about the company: LLMs can access the enterprise knowledge graph to answer employee or customer questions about products, services, or policies.
- Automate tasks: LLMs can use the knowledge graph to automate tasks, such as generating reports, summarizing documents, or routing customer inquiries.
- Personalize experiences: LLMs can personalize interactions with employees and customers by accessing relevant information from the enterprise knowledge graph.

The Right Graph for the Right Job

As you can see, there's no one-size-fits-all when it comes to knowledge graphs. The type of knowledge graph you choose will depend on the specific needs and goals of your application or LLM. By understanding the different types of knowledge graphs available, you can make informed decisions about which ones to use and how to best leverage their power.

In the next section, we'll explore the process of building and maintaining knowledge graphs, giving you a behind-the-scenes look at how these valuable resources are created and kept up-to-date.

2.4 Building and Maintaining Knowledge Graphs

Okay, so now you know what knowledge graphs are and the different types that exist. But how do you actually *build* one? It's not as simple as just throwing a bunch of facts into a pot and stirring! Creating and maintaining a knowledge graph is an ongoing process that requires careful planning, execution, and continuous improvement. Let's break it down step by step.

1. Identifying Entities and Relationships

Think of building a knowledge graph like constructing a building. You need a blueprint first, right? In this case, your blueprint is identifying the key entities and relationships you want to represent.

This involves asking questions like

- What are the core concepts in this domain?
- How are these concepts related to each other?
- What are the important attributes of each entity?

For example, if you're building a knowledge graph for Nigerian music, your entities might include

- Artists: Fela Kuti, Wizkid, Burna Boy, Tiwa Savage, etc.
- Albums: "African Giant", "Made in Lagos", "Celia", etc.
- Songs: "Ye", "Ojuelegba", "Essence", etc.
- Genres: Afrobeats, Highlife, Juju, Fuji, etc.
- Instruments: Talking drum, Kora, Saxophone, etc.

And your relationships might include

- "Fela Kuti performed the song 'Zombie'"
- "African Giant is an album by Burna Boy"

- "Afrobeats is a genre of music"
- "Wizkid is known for the genre Afrobeats"

This step requires a deep understanding of the domain you're working with. You might involve subject matter experts, analyze existing data sources, or use natural language processing (NLP) techniques to extract entities and relationships from text.

2. Collecting and Integrating Data: Gathering the Building Blocks

Once you have your blueprint, it's time to gather the building blocks – the actual data that will populate your knowledge graph. This data can come from a variety of sources

- Databases: You might have existing databases with customer information, product details, or financial records.
- Text documents: Reports, articles, web pages, and social media posts can all contain valuable information that can be extracted and added to the graph.
- APIs: You can use APIs to access real-time data from external sources, such as weather information, stock prices, or social media trends.
- Public knowledge graphs: You can leverage existing open knowledge graphs like Wikidata or DBpedia to get a head start and incorporate general knowledge into your graph.

Integrating data from these diverse sources can be challenging. You might need to convert data into a common format, resolve inconsistencies, and deal with missing or conflicting information.

3. Cleaning and Validating Data

Just like you wouldn't want to build a house with faulty materials, you don't want to build a knowledge graph with inaccurate or inconsistent data. Data quality is crucial for ensuring the reliability and usefulness of your knowledge graph.

This step involves

- Identifying and correcting errors: This might involve manual review, automated checks, or using data quality tools.
- Removing duplicates: Ensuring that each entity is represented only once in the graph.
- Handling missing data: Deciding how to deal with missing information, such as by inferring it from other data or leaving it blank.
- Validating relationships: Checking that the relationships between entities are accurate and consistent.

4. Storing and Managing the Graph

Once you have your data cleaned and validated, you need to decide how to store and manage your knowledge graph.

There are different options available, each with its own strengths and weaknesses:

- Relational databases: Traditional relational databases can be used to store knowledge graphs, but they might not be the most efficient option for handling the complex relationships and queries that are common in knowledge graphs.
- Graph databases: These databases are specifically designed for storing and querying graph-structured data. They offer high performance and scalability for knowledge graph applications.
- Triple stores: These are specialized databases that store knowledge graphs in the form of triples (subject-predicate-object), which is a common way to represent knowledge.

The choice of storage and management system will depend on the size and complexity of your knowledge graph, the types of queries you need to support, and your budget and technical expertise.

5. Updating and Evolving the Graph

The world is constantly changing, and your knowledge graph needs to keep up! This means regularly updating and evolving your graph to reflect new information, changing relationships, and emerging trends.

This might involve

- Adding new entities and relationships: As new information becomes available, you'll need to add new nodes and edges to your graph.
- Updating existing information: Keeping information up-to-date, such as correcting errors, adding new attributes, and updating relationships.
- Removing outdated information: Deleting nodes and edges that are no longer relevant or accurate.

Updating a knowledge graph can be done manually or automatically using techniques like machine learning and NLP.

Building a Knowledge Graph

Building and maintaining a knowledge graph is not a one-time task, but an ongoing journey. It requires continuous effort, attention to detail, and a willingness to adapt to changing needs and technologies. But the rewards are well worth it. A well-maintained knowledge graph can be a valuable asset for any organization or LLM application, providing a foundation for knowledge discovery, intelligent decision-making, and enhanced user experiences.

In the next chapter, we'll finally see how these knowledge graphs we've been building can be integrated with LLMs to overcome their limitations and unlock their full potential. Get ready for some exciting applications!

Chapter 3: Graph Retrieval Techniques

You now know what knowledge graphs are and how to build them. But how do we actually *use* them with LLMs? That's where graph retrieval techniques come in. Think of these techniques as the bridge connecting the structured world of knowledge graphs to the language-centric world of LLMs.

3.1 Embedding-Based Retrieval

Okay, let's explore one of the most popular and powerful techniques for retrieving information from a knowledge graph: embedding-based retrieval. This method leverages the magic of embeddings, which are essentially a way of representing entities as numerical vectors. Think of these vectors as "semantic fingerprints" that capture the meaning and relationships of entities in a multi-dimensional space.

The Essence of Embeddings

Before we get into the details of embedding-based retrieval, let's take a moment to understand what embeddings are and why they're so useful.

In essence, an embedding is a way of representing something – a word, a sentence, an image, or even a whole concept – as a point in a multi-dimensional space. The location of that point reflects the meaning and relationships of the entity it represents.

For example, the words "king" and "queen" might be represented as points that are close together in the embedding space, reflecting their similar meanings and roles. Similarly, the words "cat" and "dog" might be closer to each other than to the word "airplane," capturing their shared category of "animal."

These embeddings are typically generated using machine learning models that have been trained on massive amounts of data. These models learn to capture the semantic relationships between entities, allowing us to represent them in a way that preserves their meaning and allows for easy comparison.

How Embedding-Based Retrieval Works

Now, let's see how embedding-based retrieval uses these powerful representations to find relevant information in a knowledge graph.

1. Generate Embeddings for Entities: First, we need to generate embeddings for all the entities (nodes) in our knowledge graph. This can be done using pre-trained embedding models like Word2Vec, GloVe, or BERT, or by training our own embedding models specifically for our knowledge graph.
2. Embed the Query: When we have a query, such as "Nigerian musicians who have won Grammy awards," we also convert it into an embedding vector. This query vector represents the semantic meaning of our search.
3. Calculate Similarity: Next, we compare the query vector to the embedding vectors of all the entities in the knowledge graph. We can use various similarity measures, such as cosine similarity or Euclidean distance, to calculate how close each entity vector is to the query vector.
4. Retrieve the Most Similar Entities: Finally, we rank the entities based on their similarity scores and retrieve the top-k entities as the most relevant results for our query.

Example

Let's say we have a knowledge graph of Nigerian music, and we want to find artists similar to Fela Kuti. We would first generate embeddings for all the artists in our graph, including Fela Kuti. Then, we would embed the query "Fela Kuti" and compare it to the embeddings of other artists. The artists with the highest similarity scores, such as Burna Boy or Wizkid, would be retrieved as the most similar artists.

Advantages of Embedding-Based Retrieval

Embedding-based retrieval offers several advantages:

- Efficiency: It's computationally efficient, especially when combined with techniques like approximate nearest neighbor search, which allows for fast retrieval even in large knowledge graphs.
- Semantic Similarity: It goes beyond exact keyword matching, finding entities that are semantically similar to the query, even if they don't share the exact same words.
- Adaptability: It can be easily adapted to different domains and knowledge graphs by using appropriate embedding models.

Code Example

Python

```python
from sklearn.metrics.pairwise import
cosine_similarity




# Sample entity embeddings (replace with actual
embeddings from your knowledge graph)

entity_embeddings = {

    "Fela Kuti":,


    "Burna Boy":,
```

```python
    "Wizkid":,

    "Tiwa Savage":,

}



# Query embedding

query_embedding =  # Embedding for "Fela Kuti"



# Calculate cosine similarity

similarities = {}

for entity, embedding in
entity_embeddings.items():

    similarities[entity] =
cosine_similarity([query_embedding], [embedding])



# Sort entities by similarity

sorted_entities = sorted(similarities.items(),
key=lambda x: x, reverse=True)
```

```
# Print the top 3 most similar entities

print("Top 3 most similar entities to Fela
Kuti:")

for entity, similarity in sorted_entities[:3]:

    print(f"- {entity}: {similarity:.4f}")
```

This code snippet demonstrates how to calculate cosine similarity between a query embedding and a set of entity embeddings using the scikit-learn library in Python. You can adapt this code to your specific knowledge graph and embedding model.

Beyond Simple Similarity

While embedding-based retrieval is a powerful technique, it's important to remember that it's just one piece of the puzzle. In some cases, you might need to combine it with other techniques, such as path-based retrieval or graph neural networks, to get the most relevant and accurate results.

In the next section, we'll explore another powerful technique: path-based retrieval, which allows us to navigate the knowledge graph by following the connections between entities.

3.2 Path-Based Retrieval

Alright, let's explore another powerful technique for retrieving information from a knowledge graph: path-based retrieval. This method is all about navigating the knowledge graph by following the connections between entities, like tracing a route on a map. It's particularly useful when you're looking for specific relationships or patterns in the data, rather than just finding similar entities.

The Essence of Paths

In a knowledge graph, a path is a sequence of nodes connected by edges. It represents a chain of relationships between entities. For example, in a knowledge graph about Nigerian music, a path might connect "Fela Kuti" to "Afrobeat" through the relationship "pioneer of," and then to "Nigeria" through the relationship "originated in."

Path-based retrieval uses these paths to answer questions and find information that requires understanding the connections between entities. It's like asking, "How do I get from point A to point B?" in the knowledge graph, and the algorithm finds the best route for you.

How Path-Based Retrieval Works

The basic steps involved in path-based retrieval are:

1. Identify the Starting Node: Based on your query, you identify the starting node in the knowledge graph. For example, if you're looking for "Nigerian musicians who have won Grammy awards," your starting node might be "Nigerian musician."
2. Explore Paths: The algorithm then explores the paths emanating from the starting node, following the edges and relationships in the graph. It might follow edges related to "awards," "wins," or "achievements."
3. Match the Target Node: The algorithm looks for paths that lead to the target node, which represents the information you're looking for. In our example, the target node would be "Grammy award."
4. Retrieve Entities along the Path: Once the algorithm finds paths connecting the starting and target nodes, it retrieves

the entities (nodes) along those paths. In our example, these entities would be the Nigerian musicians who have won Grammy awards.

Example

Let's say you want to find all the artists who have collaborated with Wizkid. Using path-based retrieval, you would:

1. Start with the "Wizkid" node.
2. Follow edges labeled "collaborated with."
3. Retrieve all the artists connected to those edges.

This would give you a list of all the artists who have collaborated with Wizkid, regardless of their genre, popularity, or other attributes.

Types of Path-Finding Algorithms

There are different algorithms that can be used for path-based retrieval, each with its own strengths and weaknesses:

- Breadth-First Search (BFS): This algorithm explores the graph layer by layer, starting from the source node and expanding outwards. It's good for finding the shortest paths between entities.
- Depth-First Search (DFS): This algorithm explores the graph by going as deep as possible along each branch before backtracking. It's useful for finding all possible paths between entities.
- Dijkstra's Algorithm: This algorithm finds the shortest paths between nodes in a weighted graph, where edges have associated costs or distances. It's often used in applications like route planning and network routing.

The choice of algorithm depends on the specific query, the structure of the knowledge graph, and the desired outcome.

Advantages of Path-Based Retrieval

Path-based retrieval offers several advantages:

- Specificity: It allows you to find very specific information by following the connections in the knowledge graph.
- Relationship-centric: It focuses on the relationships between entities, making it ideal for queries that involve complex relationships or constraints.
- Explainability: The paths themselves can provide an explanation for the retrieved results, showing how the entities are connected and why they are relevant to the query.

Code Example

Python

```python
import networkx as nx




# Create a sample graph (replace with your actual
knowledge graph)

graph = nx.Graph()

graph.add_edges_from([

    ("Fela Kuti", "Afrobeat", {"label": "pioneer
of"}),

    ("Afrobeat", "Nigeria", {"label": "originated
in"}),
```

```
    ("Wizkid", "Afrobeat", {"label":
"performs"}),

])
```

```
# Find paths from "Fela Kuti" to "Nigeria"

paths = nx.all_simple_paths(graph, source="Fela
Kuti", target="Nigeria")
```

```
# Print the paths

for path in paths:

    print(path)
```

This code snippet demonstrates how to find all simple paths between two nodes in a graph using the NetworkX library in Python. You can adapt this code to your specific knowledge graph and path-finding needs.

Beyond Simple Paths

Path-based retrieval can go beyond finding simple paths between entities. It can also be used to find complex patterns, such as cycles or cliques, in the knowledge graph. This can be useful for tasks like identifying communities or clusters of related entities.

In the next section, we'll explore another powerful technique for graph retrieval: graph neural networks, which can learn directly from the structure of the knowledge graph to provide even more accurate and relevant results.

3.3 Graph Neural Networks for Retrieval

GNNs are a special breed of neural networks that are specifically designed to work with graph-structured data. They can learn directly from the connections and relationships between entities, allowing them to capture complex patterns and dependencies that might be missed by other retrieval techniques.

Why GNNs for Knowledge Graphs?

Traditional neural networks, like those used in image recognition or natural language processing, typically work with data that's organized in a grid-like structure (like pixels in an image or words in a sentence). But knowledge graphs are different. They're all about connections and relationships, and those connections are crucial for understanding the information they contain.

GNNs are built to handle this kind of interconnected data. They can "walk" the graph, passing information between connected nodes and learning how the structure of the graph influences the meaning of each entity. This allows them to capture complex dependencies and patterns that might be missed by other methods.

How GNNs Work for Retrieval

Here's a simplified breakdown of how GNNs can be used for retrieving information from a knowledge graph:

1. Encode the Graph: First, we need to convert the knowledge graph into a format that a GNN can understand. This typically involves representing each node and edge as a numerical vector, capturing its features and relationships.

2. Train the GNN: Next, we train the GNN on a retrieval task. This involves feeding it a set of queries and their corresponding relevant entities from the knowledge graph. The GNN learns to predict the relevance of entities to a given query by analyzing the graph structure and the features of the entities.
3. Use the Trained GNN for Retrieval: Once the GNN is trained, we can use it to retrieve relevant entities for new queries. We simply feed the query to the GNN, and it predicts which entities in the knowledge graph are most relevant.

Example

Let's say you're building a music recommendation system using a knowledge graph. You could use a GNN to learn the complex relationships between artists, albums, songs, genres, and user preferences. The GNN could then be used to recommend new music to users based on their listening history and the connections in the knowledge graph.

Advantages of GNNs for Retrieval

GNNs offer several advantages for knowledge graph retrieval:

- Capturing Complex Relationships: They can capture complex dependencies and patterns in the graph structure, going beyond simple pairwise relationships.
- Learning from the Whole Graph: They can learn from the entire graph, considering the global context of each entity.
- Adaptability: They can be adapted to different knowledge graphs and retrieval tasks by adjusting their architecture and training data.

Popular GNN Architectures

There are various GNN architectures that can be used for retrieval, each with its own strengths and weaknesses:

- Graph Convolutional Networks (GCNs): These are a popular type of GNN that learn by aggregating information from neighboring nodes.
- Graph Attention Networks (GATs): These GNNs use attention mechanisms to focus on the most relevant neighbors when aggregating information.
- GraphSAGE: This architecture is designed to be scalable to large graphs by sampling neighbors during training.

The choice of architecture depends on the specific task and the characteristics of the knowledge graph.

Code Example

Python

```python
import torch

from torch_geometric.nn import GCNConv

from torch_geometric.data import Data



# Define a simple GCN model

class GCN(torch.nn.Module):

    def __init__(self):
```

```python
        super().__init__()

        self.conv1 = GCNConv(in_channels=1433,
out_channels=16)

        self.conv2 = GCNConv(in_channels=16,
out_channels=7)


    def forward(self, data):

        x, edge_index = data.x, data.edge_index

        x = self.conv1(x, edge_index)

        x = torch.relu(x)

        x = torch.dropout(x,
training=self.training)

        x = self.conv2(x, edge_index)

        return torch.sigmoid(x)


# Create a sample graph (replace with your actual
knowledge graph)

edge_index = torch.tensor([,
```

```python
                        ], dtype=torch.long)

x = torch.randn(3, 1433)   # Example node features

data = Data(x=x, edge_index=edge_index)


# Instantiate and train the GCN model

model = GCN()

optimizer = torch.optim.Adam(model.parameters(),
lr=0.01)

criterion = torch.nn.BCELoss()


for epoch in range(200):

    optimizer.zero_grad()

    out = model(data)

    loss = criterion(out, torch.randn(3, 7))   #
Example target labels

    loss.backward()

    optimizer.step()
```

```
# Use the trained model for retrieval (example)

query_embedding = torch.randn(1, 1433)

query_data = Data(x=query_embedding,
edge_index=edge_index)

predicted_relevance = model(query_data)
```

This code snippet demonstrates a basic implementation of a GCN model for graph retrieval using the PyTorch Geometric library. You can adapt this code to your specific knowledge graph and retrieval task.

GNNs

GNNs are a powerful tool for retrieving information from knowledge graphs, offering a way to capture complex relationships and learn directly from the structure of the data. As research in this area continues to advance, we can expect GNNs to play an even greater role in enhancing the capabilities of LLMs and enabling new and exciting applications.

In the next section, we'll discuss some important considerations for ensuring the efficiency and scalability of graph retrieval techniques, especially when dealing with large knowledge graphs.

3.4 Graph Neural Networks for Retrieval

GNNs are a special breed of neural networks that are specifically designed to work with graph-structured data. They can learn directly from the connections and relationships between entities, allowing them to capture complex patterns and dependencies that might be missed by other retrieval techniques.

Why GNNs for Knowledge Graphs?

Traditional neural networks, like those used in image recognition or natural language processing, typically work with data that's organized in a grid-like structure (like pixels in an image or words in a sentence). But knowledge graphs are different. They're all about connections and relationships, and those connections are crucial for understanding the information they contain.

GNNs are built to handle this kind of interconnected data. They can "walk" the graph, passing information between connected nodes and learning how the structure of the graph influences the meaning of each entity. This allows them to capture complex dependencies and patterns that might be missed by other methods.

How GNNs Work for Retrieval

Here's a simplified breakdown of how GNNs can be used for retrieving information from a knowledge graph:

1. Encode the Graph: First, we need to convert the knowledge graph into a format that a GNN can understand. This typically involves representing each node and edge as a numerical vector, capturing its features and relationships.
2. Train the GNN: Next, we train the GNN on a retrieval task. This involves feeding it a set of queries and their corresponding relevant entities from the knowledge graph. The GNN learns to predict the relevance of entities to a given query by analyzing the graph structure and the features of the entities.
3. Use the Trained GNN for Retrieval: Once the GNN is trained, we can use it to retrieve relevant entities for new queries. We simply feed the query to the GNN, and it

predicts which entities in the knowledge graph are most relevant.

Example

Let's say you're building a music recommendation system using a knowledge graph. You could use a GNN to learn the complex relationships between artists, albums, songs, genres, and user preferences. The GNN could then be used to recommend new music to users based on their listening history and the connections in the knowledge graph.

Advantages of GNNs for Retrieval

GNNs offer several advantages for knowledge graph retrieval:

- Capturing Complex Relationships: They can capture complex dependencies and patterns in the graph structure, going beyond simple pairwise relationships.
- Learning from the Whole Graph: They can learn from the entire graph, considering the global context of each entity.
- Adaptability: They can be adapted to different knowledge graphs and retrieval tasks by adjusting their architecture and training data.

Popular GNN Architectures

There are various GNN architectures that can be used for retrieval, each with its own strengths and weaknesses:

- Graph Convolutional Networks (GCNs): These are a popular type of GNN that learn by aggregating information from neighboring nodes.
- Graph Attention Networks (GATs): These GNNs use attention mechanisms to focus on the most relevant neighbors when aggregating information.
- GraphSAGE: This architecture is designed to be scalable to large graphs by sampling neighbors during training.

The choice of architecture depends on the specific task and the characteristics of the knowledge graph.

Code Example

Python

```
import torch

from torch_geometric.nn import GCNConv

from torch_geometric.data import Data



# Define a simple GCN model

class GCN(torch.nn.Module):

    def __init__(self):

        super().__init__()

        self.conv1 = GCNConv(in_channels=1433,
out_channels=16)

        self.conv2 = GCNConv(in_channels=16,
out_channels=7)


    def forward(self, data):
```

```python
        x, edge_index = data.x, data.edge_index

        x = self.conv1(x, edge_index)

        x = torch.relu(x)

        x = torch.dropout(x,
training=self.training)

        x = self.conv2(x, edge_index)

        return torch.sigmoid(x)



# Create a sample graph (replace with your actual
knowledge graph)

edge_index = torch.tensor([,

                          ], dtype=torch.long)

x = torch.randn(3, 1433)   # Example node features

data = Data(x=x, edge_index=edge_index)



# Instantiate and train the GCN model

model = GCN()
```

```python
optimizer = torch.optim.Adam(model.parameters(),
lr=0.01)

criterion = torch.nn.BCELoss()


for epoch in range(200):

    optimizer.zero_grad()

    out = model(data)

    loss = criterion(out, torch.randn(3, 7))  #
Example target labels

    loss.backward()

    optimizer.step()


# Use the trained model for retrieval (example)

query_embedding = torch.randn(1, 1433)

query_data = Data(x=query_embedding,
edge_index=edge_index)

predicted_relevance = model(query_data)
```

This code snippet demonstrates a basic implementation of a GCN model for graph retrieval using the PyTorch Geometric library. You can adapt this code to your specific knowledge graph and retrieval task.

GNNs

GNNs are a powerful tool for retrieving information from knowledge graphs, offering a way to capture complex relationships and learn directly from the structure of the data. As research in this area continues to advance, we can expect GNNs to play an even greater role in enhancing the capabilities of LLMs and enabling new and exciting applications.

In the next section, we'll discuss some important considerations for ensuring the efficiency and scalability of graph retrieval techniques, especially when dealing with large knowledge graphs.

Chapter 4: Enhancing LLM Capabilities with Graph Retrieval

Alright, it's time to bring it all together! We've explored the limitations of LLMs, delved into the world of knowledge graphs, and learned about various graph retrieval techniques. Now, let's see how this powerful combination can be used to enhance LLM capabilities and address their shortcomings. Get ready to witness the magic of knowledge-enhanced LLMs!

4.1 Improved Factual Accuracy and Knowledge Grounding

One of the most exciting aspects of combining LLMs with knowledge graphs is the potential to significantly boost their factual accuracy. Think about it: LLMs, for all their linguistic prowess, can sometimes be a bit like that friend who loves to tell a good story, but occasionally embellishes the details or gets things mixed up. Knowledge graphs, on the other hand, are like a meticulously researched encyclopedia, offering a reliable source of truth.

By connecting LLMs to knowledge graphs, we can essentially give them a fact-checking superpower. This opens up a whole range of possibilities for making LLMs more trustworthy and dependable sources of information.

How Knowledge Graphs Ground LLMs in Facts

Let's break down how this works in practice:

1. Verification: Before an LLM confidently declares that "Nigeria's capital is Lagos" (which, as you know, is incorrect!), we can use graph retrieval to quickly check that statement against the knowledge graph. If the graph

correctly states that "Abuja is the capital of Nigeria," the LLM can be prompted to revise its output. This prevents the spread of misinformation and ensures that the LLM's responses are grounded in verified facts.

2. Evidence and Explainability: Not only can we use knowledge graphs to verify facts, but we can also use them to provide evidence for the LLM's claims. Imagine asking an LLM, "Who wrote Things Fall Apart?" Instead of just getting the answer "Chinua Achebe," you could also get a link to the relevant node in the knowledge graph, showing the connection between the author and the book. This adds a layer of transparency and allows users to understand where the information is coming from.

3. Generating More Grounded Responses: By incorporating factual information from the knowledge graph directly into the LLM's output, we can create responses that are inherently more grounded and less prone to hallucinations. For example, an LLM could generate a summary of Nigerian history, pulling key dates and events directly from the knowledge graph to ensure accuracy.

Real-World Applications

This ability to improve factual accuracy has huge implications for a wide range of applications:

- Customer service: Imagine a customer service chatbot that can accurately answer questions about products, services, or company policies by accessing a knowledge graph. This would lead to more efficient and satisfying customer interactions.
- Education: LLMs could be used to create personalized learning experiences, adapting to a student's knowledge level and providing accurate information and explanations from a knowledge graph.
- Journalism and content creation: LLMs could assist journalists and writers by generating fact-checked articles

and reports, ensuring that the information presented is accurate and supported by evidence.

- Scientific research: LLMs could help researchers analyze scientific literature, identify relevant studies, and extract key findings, all while being grounded in the factual knowledge of a scientific knowledge graph.

Example

Let's say you're building a system to fact-check news articles. You could use an LLM to generate a summary of the article and then use graph retrieval to compare the claims in the summary to a knowledge graph of verified information. Any discrepancies could then be flagged for further investigation.

Code Example

Python

```python
# Sample knowledge graph (replace with your
actual knowledge graph)

knowledge_graph = {

    "Nigeria": {"capital": "Abuja"},

    "Ghana": {"capital": "Accra"},

}



# LLM output (potentially inaccurate)
```

```python
llm_output = "The capital of Nigeria is Lagos."


# Extract the claim from the LLM output

claim = llm_output.split(" is ")  # ["The capital
of Nigeria", "Lagos."]



# Verify the claim against the knowledge graph

entity = claim.replace("The capital of ", "")  #
"Nigeria"

true_value = knowledge_graph.get(entity,
{}).get("capital")  # "Abuja"



# Check if the claim is accurate

if claim.rstrip(".") == true_value:

    print("The claim is accurate.")

else:

    print(f"The claim is inaccurate. The correct
capital is {true_value}.")
```

This code snippet demonstrates a simple way to verify a claim extracted from an LLM's output against a knowledge graph. You can adapt this code to your specific needs and knowledge graph structure.

The Importance of Grounded LLMs

As LLMs become more prevalent in our lives, ensuring their factual accuracy is becoming increasingly important. By grounding LLMs in the knowledge of knowledge graphs, we can create more trustworthy and reliable AI systems that can be used to inform, educate, and assist us in various aspects of our lives.

In the next section, we'll explore how knowledge graphs can also enhance the common sense reasoning capabilities of LLMs, helping them understand the world in a more human-like way.

4.2 Enhanced Common Sense Reasoning

It's something we humans often take for granted. We know that you can't walk through walls, that objects fall when dropped, and that people generally don't eat rocks. But for LLMs, these seemingly simple concepts can be surprisingly challenging. It's like they have a vast library of knowledge but haven't quite grasped the basic rules of how the world works.

This lack of common sense reasoning is a major hurdle for LLMs, preventing them from truly understanding the world and generating outputs that are consistently grounded in reality. Luckily, knowledge graphs can help address this by providing LLMs with a structured representation of common sense knowledge.

How Knowledge Graphs Bring Common Sense to LLMs

Think of a knowledge graph as a network of interconnected concepts and rules. It can capture common sense knowledge in the form of relationships and constraints. For example, a knowledge graph might contain the rule that "all birds can fly" or the constraint that "a person cannot be in two places at the same time."

By connecting LLMs to knowledge graphs, we can enable them to:

1. Validate their outputs: Before an LLM generates a response, it can consult the knowledge graph to check whether its output is consistent with common sense knowledge. This can prevent it from making illogical statements or generating scenarios that defy basic physics or logic.
2. Reason more effectively: LLMs can use the rules and relationships in the knowledge graph to make inferences and draw conclusions. For example, if an LLM knows that "all birds can fly" and that "a penguin is a bird," it can infer that "a penguin can fly" (even though we know that's not entirely true in the real world).
3. Generate more plausible responses: By incorporating common sense knowledge from the knowledge graph, LLMs can generate responses that are more grounded in reality and less likely to contain nonsensical or illogical elements.

Real-World Examples

This ability to enhance common sense reasoning has significant implications for various applications

- Story generation: LLMs can use common sense knowledge to generate more believable and engaging stories, avoiding plot holes or unrealistic scenarios.
- Dialogue systems: Chatbots and conversational agents can use common sense to understand user requests, respond appropriately, and avoid making nonsensical statements.
- Robotics: Robots equipped with LLMs can use common sense knowledge to navigate the physical world, interact with objects, and avoid dangerous situations.

Example

Let's say you're building a system to help children learn about the world. You could use an LLM to generate stories and explanations, and then use a knowledge graph to ensure that the information presented is consistent with common sense knowledge. This would help children develop a more accurate and grounded understanding of the world around them.

Code Example

Python

```python
# Sample knowledge graph with common sense rules
(replace with your actual knowledge graph)

knowledge_graph = {

    "rules": [

        {"if": "someone is swimming", "then":
"they are in water"},

        {"if": "something is on fire", "then":
"it is hot"},

    ]

}



# LLM output
```

```
llm_output = "The man was swimming in the
desert."
```

Extract the situation from the LLM output

```
situation = "someone is swimming"  # Simplified
for this example
```

Check if the situation violates any common sense rules

```
for rule in knowledge_graph["rules"]:

    if rule["if"] == situation and "in water" not
in llm_output:

        print("The LLM output violates a common
sense rule.")

        break

else:

    print("The LLM output is consistent with
common sense rules.")
```

This code snippet demonstrates a simple way to check whether an LLM's output violates any common sense rules defined in a knowledge graph. You can adapt this code to your specific needs and knowledge graph structure.

The Importance of Common Sense in LLMs

Common sense reasoning is a fundamental aspect of human intelligence, and it's crucial for building LLMs that can truly understand and interact with the world in a meaningful way. By incorporating common sense knowledge from knowledge graphs, we can create more grounded, reliable, and trustworthy AI systems that can be used to solve real-world problems and enhance our lives.

In the next section, we'll explore how knowledge graphs can also improve the contextual understanding and coherence of LLMs, allowing them to engage in more meaningful and consistent conversations.

4.3 Better Contextual Understanding and Coherence

You know how in a conversation, you don't just focus on the last sentence someone said, but you consider the whole flow of the discussion? You remember what was said earlier, who said it, and how it all connects together. Well, that's contextual understanding, and it's something that LLMs can sometimes struggle with.

Think of it like this: LLMs can be a bit like goldfish, with a limited memory of what just happened. They might respond perfectly to your last sentence, but completely forget what you were talking about five minutes ago. This can lead to conversations that feel disjointed, contradictory, or just plain confusing.

But don't worry, knowledge graphs are here to help! By connecting LLMs to knowledge graphs, we can give them a much-needed boost in contextual understanding and coherence.

How Knowledge Graphs Enhance Context

Knowledge graphs are all about connections. They represent not just individual entities, but also the relationships between them. This interconnectedness provides valuable context for LLMs, allowing them to:

1. Track entities and relationships: Imagine you're having a conversation about Nigerian history, and you mention "the Biafran War." A knowledge graph can help the LLM understand that this refers to a specific conflict that occurred in Nigeria between 1967 and 1970, and it can access information about the key players, events, and consequences of the war. This allows the LLM to generate more informed and relevant responses.
2. Maintain coherence over longer interactions: By remembering the entities and relationships mentioned earlier in the conversation, LLMs can avoid contradictions, stay on topic, and generate responses that build on previous turns. This creates a more natural and engaging conversational experience.
3. Understand the flow of information: Knowledge graphs can help LLMs understand how different pieces of information relate to each other, allowing them to follow the logical progression of a conversation or document and generate responses that are consistent with the overall context.

Real-World Examples

This enhanced contextual understanding has significant benefits for various applications:

- Chatbots and conversational agents: Knowledge graphs can help chatbots maintain a consistent persona, remember user preferences, and provide more relevant and helpful responses.
- Personalized learning: LLMs can use knowledge graphs to tailor educational content to a student's individual needs

and learning style, providing a more engaging and effective learning experience.

- Content creation: LLMs can generate more coherent and contextually relevant articles, stories, and reports by leveraging the information in a knowledge graph.

Example

Let's say you're building a chatbot for a museum. You could use a knowledge graph to represent information about the museum's exhibits, artists, and historical periods. This would allow the chatbot to answer visitor questions in a contextually relevant way, providing information about specific exhibits or artists based on the visitor's location or previous interactions.

Code Example

Python

```python
# Sample knowledge graph (replace with your
actual knowledge graph)

knowledge_graph = {

    "Nigeria": {"capital": "Abuja", "continent":
"Africa"},

    "Abuja": {"country": "Nigeria", "population":
"6 million"},

}
```

```python
# User query

user_query = "What is the population of the
capital of Nigeria?"



# Extract entities from the query

entities = ["Nigeria", "capital", "population"]



# Retrieve relevant information from the
knowledge graph

context = {}

for entity in entities:

    if entity in knowledge_graph:

        context.update(knowledge_graph[entity])



# Generate a response using the context

response = f"The population of
{context['capital']}, the capital of {entities},
is {context['population']}."
```

```
# Print the response
```

```
print(response)   # Output: The population of
Abuja, the capital of Nigeria, is 6 million.
```

This code snippet demonstrates how to use a knowledge graph to extract relevant context for a user query and generate a more informed and contextualized response. You can adapt this code to your specific needs and knowledge graph structure.

The Importance of Context for LLMs

Contextual understanding is a crucial aspect of human communication, and it's essential for building LLMs that can truly engage in meaningful and coherent interactions. By leveraging the power of knowledge graphs, we can enhance the contextual awareness of LLMs, making them more valuable and trustworthy partners in communication, learning, and problem-solving.

In the next section, we'll explore how knowledge graphs can also improve the explainability and interpretability of LLMs, making them more transparent and trustworthy.

4.4 Explainability and Interpretability

When you ask a friend for advice, you not only want a good answer, but you also want to understand *why* they're giving you that advice. What's their reasoning? What factors did they consider? The same goes for LLMs. As these models become more powerful and integrated into our lives, it's crucial that we can understand how they arrive at their conclusions.

This is where explainability and interpretability come in. Explainability refers to the ability to understand *why* an LLM generates a particular output, while interpretability refers to the ability to understand *how* the LLM works internally. Think of it like this: explainability is like getting a clear explanation from your friend about their advice, while interpretability is like being able to peek inside their brain and see their thought process.

LLMs, especially the larger and more complex ones, can often feel like "black boxes." We feed them input, they produce output, but the internal workings remain mysterious. This lack of transparency can be a barrier to trust and adoption, especially in critical applications like healthcare or finance.

How Knowledge Graphs Shed Light on LLM Decisions

Thankfully, knowledge graphs can help shed light on the inner workings of LLMs and make their decisions more transparent.

Here's how:

1. Tracing the Reasoning Path: When an LLM uses a knowledge graph to answer a question or generate a response, we can trace the path through the graph that led to that output. This path reveals the connections and relationships that the LLM used to arrive at its conclusion, providing valuable insights into its reasoning process.
2. Identifying Supporting Evidence: Knowledge graphs can also help us identify the specific pieces of evidence that an LLM used to support its claims. This allows us to verify the accuracy of the information and understand the basis for the LLM's decision.
3. Providing Contextual Information: By linking LLM outputs to relevant entities and relationships in the knowledge graph, we can provide additional context and background information that helps explain the LLM's reasoning.

Real-World Examples

This increased explainability and interpretability has important implications for various applications:

- Medical diagnosis: If an LLM is used to assist with medical diagnosis, it's crucial to understand why it recommends a particular treatment or diagnosis. Knowledge graphs can provide a clear explanation of the reasoning behind the LLM's recommendations, increasing trust and allowing doctors to make informed decisions.
- Financial analysis: In financial applications, it's essential to understand how an LLM arrived at a particular investment strategy or risk assessment. Knowledge graphs can help explain the factors that the LLM considered, making its decisions more transparent and accountable.
- Legal applications: LLMs can be used to analyze legal documents and provide insights, but it's important to understand how they arrived at their conclusions. Knowledge graphs can help trace the legal reasoning and precedents that the LLM used, ensuring that its outputs are grounded in legal principles.

Example

Let's say you're using an LLM-powered movie recommendation system. Instead of just getting a list of movies, you also get an explanation of why each movie was recommended.

The explanation might say something like:

"We recommend 'The Matrix' because you enjoyed 'Inception,' and both movies share the themes of reality bending and artificial intelligence. They also both feature strong female characters and have high ratings on IMDB."

This explanation, based on connections in a knowledge graph, helps you understand the LLM's reasoning and makes the recommendation more trustworthy and personalized.

Code Example

Python

```python
import networkx as nx




# Sample knowledge graph (replace with your
actual knowledge graph)

graph = nx.Graph()

graph.add_edges_from([

    ("Chinua Achebe", "Things Fall Apart",
{"label": "wrote"}),

    ("Things Fall Apart", "Colonialism",
{"label": "theme"}),

    ("Things Fall Apart", "Nigeria", {"label":
"setting"}),

])
```

```python
# LLM output

llm_output = "Chinua Achebe wrote Things Fall
Apart, a novel about colonialism set in Nigeria."



# Extract entities from the LLM output

entities = ["Chinua Achebe", "Things Fall Apart",
"Colonialism", "Nigeria"]



# Find paths between entities in the knowledge
graph

paths =

for i in range(len(entities) - 1):

    for j in range(i + 1, len(entities)):

        path = nx.shortest_path(graph,
source=entities[i], target=entities[j])

        paths.append(path)



# Print the paths
```

```
print("Reasoning paths:")

for path in paths:

    print(path)
```

This code snippet demonstrates how to extract reasoning paths from a knowledge graph based on entities mentioned in an LLM's output. This can provide insights into the LLM's decision-making process and make its outputs more explainable.

The Importance of Explainable LLMs

As LLMs become more integrated into our lives, it's crucial that we can understand and trust their decisions. Knowledge graphs offer a powerful way to enhance the explainability and interpretability of LLMs, making them more transparent and accountable. This is essential for building trust in AI systems and ensuring that they are used responsibly and ethically.

In the next chapter, we'll explore some of the exciting applications of graph-powered LLMs and see how they're already making a difference in various fields.

Chapter 5: Applications of Graph-Powered LLMs

We've spent a good amount of time understanding the nuts and bolts, but now it's time to explore how this technology is actually being used to solve real-world problems and create some pretty amazing applications.

5.1 Question Answering and Information Retrieval

Alright, let's explore one of the most impactful applications of graph-powered LLMs: revolutionizing how we find and access information. Think about how you typically search for information online. You type in some keywords, and you get back a list of web pages, right? But what if, instead of sifting through those pages yourself, you could just ask a question and get a direct, accurate answer, along with all the relevant context and supporting evidence? That's the promise of graph-powered LLMs for question answering and information retrieval.

Traditional Search vs. Knowledge-Enhanced Search

Traditional search engines rely heavily on keyword matching.[1] They look for pages that contain the words in your query, but they don't truly understand the *meaning* of those words or the relationships between them. This can lead to irrelevant results, especially for complex or nuanced questions.[2]

Graph-powered LLMs, on the other hand, can tap into the knowledge and structure of a knowledge graph to provide a much richer and more intelligent search experience.[3]

Here's how it works:

1. Understanding the Question: When you ask a question, the LLM doesn't just look for keywords.[4] It uses its natural language understanding capabilities to analyze the structure and intent of your question.[5] It figures out what entities are involved, what relationships you're interested in, and what kind of answer you're looking for.

2. Retrieving Relevant Information: The LLM then uses graph retrieval techniques to find the most relevant information in the knowledge graph.[6] This might involve finding specific entities, traversing relationships, or even performing complex reasoning over the graph.

3. Generating a Comprehensive Answer: Finally, the LLM combines its language generation skills with the retrieved knowledge to generate a comprehensive and informative answer to your question.[7] This answer might include direct answers to your questions, relevant context from the knowledge graph, and links to supporting evidence.

Example:

Let's say you're researching the Nigerian Civil War and you ask the question: "What were the key factors that led to the conflict?"

A traditional search engine might give you a list of web pages about the war, but you'd have to read through them yourself to find the specific information you're looking for.

A graph-powered LLM, on the other hand, could provide a direct answer like:

"The Nigerian Civil War, also known as the Biafran War, was primarily caused by a complex interplay of political, economic, and ethnic factors.[8] These included the First Republic's political instability, economic disparities between regions, and ethnic tensions between the Igbo, Hausa, and Yoruba people. The 1966 coups, which led to the assassination of several political leaders, further exacerbated these tensions and ultimately triggered the conflict."

This answer not only provides a concise summary of the key factors but also links them to relevant entities in the knowledge graph, such as the "First Republic," "Igbo people," and "1966 coups." This allows you to easily explore related information and gain a deeper understanding of the topic.

Benefits of Knowledge-Enhanced Question Answering

This approach to question answering offers several advantages:

- Accuracy: By grounding answers in a knowledge graph, we can ensure that the information provided is accurate and reliable.
- Relevance: The LLM can identify the most relevant information for the specific question, avoiding irrelevant or redundant results.[9]
- Completeness: The answer can include not just a direct answer but also relevant context and supporting evidence, providing a more comprehensive understanding.
- Explainability: The LLM can explain how it arrived at the answer by showing the connections and relationships in the knowledge graph that were used.

Real-World Applications

This technology has the potential to transform how we access and interact with information in various domains:

- Education: Students can ask questions and get personalized answers tailored to their learning level and needs.[10]
- Customer service: Customers can get quick and accurate answers to their questions about products or services.[11]

- Healthcare: Doctors and patients can access reliable medical information and get answers to complex health questions.[12]
- Research: Researchers can quickly find relevant information and explore complex topics by asking questions and getting comprehensive answers.

Code Example

Python

```python
# Sample knowledge graph (replace with your
actual knowledge graph)

knowledge_graph = {

    "Nigeria": {"capital": "Abuja", "continent":
"Africa"},

    "Abuja": {"country": "Nigeria", "population":
"6 million"},

}




# User question

user_question = "What is the capital of Nigeria?"




# Extract entities from the question
```

```
entities = ["Nigeria", "capital"]


# Retrieve the answer from the knowledge graph

answer = knowledge_graph.get(entities,
{}).get(entities)



# Generate a response

if answer:

    response = f"The capital of {entities} is
{answer}."

else:

    response = "I couldn't find the answer to
your question."



# Print the response

print(response)   # Output: The capital of Nigeria
is Abuja.
```

This code snippet demonstrates a simple way to build a question answering system using a knowledge graph. You can adapt this code to your specific needs and knowledge graph structure.

The Future of Knowledge-Enhanced Search

As LLMs and knowledge graphs continue to evolve, we can expect even more sophisticated and powerful question answering systems to emerge. These systems will be able to understand complex questions, reason over vast amounts of knowledge, and provide personalized and insightful answers. This will transform how we learn, make decisions, and interact with the world around us.

In the next section, we'll explore another exciting application of graph-powered LLMs: conversational AI and dialogue systems.

5.2 Conversational AI and Dialogue Systems

Alright, let's talk about chatbots. You've probably interacted with them before, whether it's on a website, through a messaging app, or even with a virtual assistant like Siri or Alexa. But let's be honest, sometimes those conversations can feel a bit... clunky. The chatbot might misunderstand your requests, forget what you just said, or give you irrelevant information.[1]

That's because traditional chatbots often rely on simple rule-based systems or basic machine learning models that lack a deeper understanding of language and context.[2] But don't worry, graph-powered LLMs are here to change that! They can help us build conversational AI systems that are more engaging, informative, and truly understand what we're saying.[3]

How Knowledge Graphs Enhance Conversations

By incorporating knowledge graphs into conversational AI systems, we can:

1. Maintain Context and Memory: Remember how we talked about LLMs sometimes having a "goldfish memory"? Well, knowledge graphs can help with that! They can store information about the ongoing conversation, including previous turns, user preferences, and relevant entities.[4] This allows the chatbot to maintain context, avoid contradictions, and generate responses that are consistent with the flow of the conversation.[5]

2. Understand User Intent: Knowledge graphs can also help chatbots understand the user's underlying intent, even if it's not explicitly stated.[6] For example, if you ask a chatbot "What's the weather like in Lagos today?", it can use a knowledge graph to understand that you're interested in the current weather conditions in Lagos, even if you don't explicitly say "current" or "today."

3. Provide Personalized Responses: By accessing user information and preferences stored in the knowledge graph, chatbots can tailor their responses and recommendations to individual users.[7] This creates a more personalized and engaging experience.

4. Engage in Multi-Turn Conversations: Knowledge graphs can help chatbots engage in more complex and multi-turn conversations, remembering previous interactions and building on them to provide more relevant and informative responses.[8]

Real-World Examples

This enhanced conversational ability has significant implications for various applications:

- Customer service: Imagine a customer service chatbot that can understand your specific problem, access your account information, and provide personalized solutions. This would lead to more efficient and satisfying customer interactions.

- Healthcare: Chatbots can be used to provide patients with medical information, answer their questions, and even schedule appointments.[9] Knowledge graphs can help these chatbots understand complex medical terminology and provide accurate and relevant information.[10]
- Education: Educational chatbots can engage students in interactive conversations, provide personalized feedback and guidance, and even adapt to different learning styles.[11]
- Entertainment: Chatbots can be used to create interactive games, tell stories, and provide personalized entertainment experiences.[12]

Example

Let's say you're building a chatbot to help people plan their trips. You could use a knowledge graph to represent information about destinations, flights, hotels, attractions, and user preferences.

This would allow the chatbot to:

- Understand user travel goals: The chatbot could ask questions like "Where do you want to go?" and "What are your interests?" to understand the user's travel preferences.
- Provide personalized recommendations: Based on the user's preferences and the information in the knowledge graph, the chatbot could recommend destinations, flights, hotels, and activities.[13]
- Answer user questions: The chatbot could answer questions about specific destinations, such as "What is the weather like in Bali in June?" or "What are the must-see attractions in Paris?"
- Book flights and hotels: The chatbot could even help users book flights and hotels directly through the conversation.

Code Example

Python

```python
# Sample knowledge graph (replace with your
actual knowledge graph)

knowledge_graph = {

    "user": {"name": "Alice", "location":
"Lagos", "interests": ["music", "art"]},

    "Lagos": {"country": "Nigeria",
"attractions": ["National Museum", "Lekki
Conservation Centre"]},

    "music": {"genres": ["Afrobeats",
"Highlife"], "artists": ["Fela Kuti", "Wizkid"]},

}


# User query

user_query = "I'm interested in music. What can I
do in Lagos?"
```

```python
# Access user context from the knowledge graph

user_interests =
knowledge_graph["user"]["interests"]

location = knowledge_graph["user"]["location"]



# Retrieve relevant information from the
knowledge graph

if "music" in user_interests:

    music_info = knowledge_graph["music"]

    attractions =
knowledge_graph[location]["attractions"]

    response = f"Since you're interested in
music, you might enjoy exploring the
{music_info['genres']} scene in {location}. You
could also check out these attractions: {',
'.join(attractions)}."

else:

    response = "I'm not sure what you'd enjoy in
Lagos. Can you tell me more about your
interests?"
```

```
# Print the response
```

```
print(response)
```

This code snippet demonstrates how to use a knowledge graph to access user context and generate more relevant and personalized responses in a conversational AI system. You can adapt this code to your specific needs and knowledge graph structure.

The Future of Conversational AI

Graph-powered LLMs are paving the way for a new generation of conversational AI systems that are more human-like, engaging, and helpful. As the technology continues to evolve, we can expect chatbots to become even more sophisticated, seamlessly integrating into our lives and assisting us with various tasks, from answering questions and providing information to making recommendations and even offering emotional support.

5.3 Recommendation Systems

Have you ever wondered how streaming services like Netflix or Spotify seem to know exactly what movies or music you'll enjoy? Or how online stores like Amazon seem to suggest products that perfectly match your interests? That's the magic of recommendation systems, and graph-powered LLMs are taking them to a whole new level.

Traditional recommendation systems often rely on simple techniques like collaborative filtering (finding users with similar tastes) or content-based filtering (analyzing the attributes of items). While these methods can be effective, they have limitations. They might recommend items that are too similar to what you've already seen or miss out on hidden gems that you might love.

Graph-powered LLMs, on the other hand, can leverage the rich knowledge and connections in a knowledge graph to provide more personalized, diverse, and insightful recommendations. Let's see how they do it.

How Knowledge Graphs Enhance Recommendations

By incorporating knowledge graphs into recommendation systems, we can:

1. Understand User Preferences More Deeply: Knowledge graphs can capture a wealth of information about users, including their demographics, interests, purchase history, and social connections. This allows LLMs to build a more comprehensive understanding of each user's preferences, going beyond simple ratings or purchase history.

2. Identify Relevant Connections: Knowledge graphs can reveal hidden connections between items that might not be obvious based on traditional methods. For example, a knowledge graph might connect a book you've enjoyed to other books by the same author, books with similar themes, or even books that are popular among people with similar interests to yours.

3. Provide Personalized Explanations: LLMs can use the knowledge graph to explain why they're recommending a particular item. This explanation might highlight specific features of the item that match your preferences, connections to other items you've liked, or even social connections with other users who have enjoyed the item.

4. Generate Diverse Recommendations: Knowledge graphs can help LLMs avoid the "filter bubble" effect, where you only see recommendations for things that are similar to what you've already liked. By exploring different paths and connections in the knowledge graph, LLMs can suggest a wider range of items that you might find interesting, expanding your horizons and introducing you to new things.

Real-World Examples

This enhanced recommendation capability has significant implications for various applications:

- E-commerce: Online stores can use graph-powered LLMs to recommend products that are more likely to be relevant to each customer, increasing sales and customer satisfaction.
- Streaming services: Streaming services like Netflix and Spotify can use knowledge graphs to recommend movies, TV shows, and music that better match user preferences, leading to increased engagement and retention.
- Personalized learning: Educational platforms can use knowledge graphs to recommend learning resources, courses, and activities that are tailored to each student's learning goals and preferences.
- Social networks: Social networks can use knowledge graphs to recommend connections, groups, and events that are relevant to each user's interests and social circles.

Example

Let's say you're building a book recommendation system for a library. You could use a knowledge graph to represent information about books, authors, genres, themes, and user reading history.

This would allow the LLM to:

- Understand user reading preferences: The LLM could analyze user reading history and connect it to information about books and authors in the knowledge graph to understand their preferences for specific genres, themes, and writing styles.
- Identify relevant connections: The LLM could use the knowledge graph to find connections between books that

might not be obvious, such as books by authors with similar styles or books that share common themes.

- Provide personalized explanations: The LLM could explain why it's recommending a particular book, highlighting specific features that match the user's preferences or connections to other books they've enjoyed.
- Generate diverse recommendations: The LLM could explore different paths and connections in the knowledge graph to recommend a variety of books, including new releases, hidden gems, and books outside the user's usual genres.

Code Example

Python

```
# Sample knowledge graph (replace with your
actual knowledge graph)

knowledge_graph = {

    "user": {"name": "Bob", "preferences":
["science fiction", "fantasy"]},

    "science fiction": {"books": ["Dune",
"Foundation", "The Martian"]},

    "fantasy": {"books": ["The Lord of the
Rings", "Harry Potter", "A Song of Ice and
Fire"]},

}
```

```python
# Get user preferences from the knowledge graph

user_preferences =
knowledge_graph["user"]["preferences"]


# Recommend books based on user preferences

recommendations =

for preference in user_preferences:


recommendations.extend(knowledge_graph[preference
]["books"])


# Print the recommendations

print("Recommended books:")

for book in recommendations:

    print(book)
```

This code snippet demonstrates a simple way to recommend books based on user preferences stored in a knowledge graph. You can adapt this code to your specific needs and knowledge graph structure.

The Future of Recommendation Systems

Graph-powered LLMs are revolutionizing recommendation systems, making them more personalized, diverse, and explainable. As the technology continues to evolve, we can expect even more sophisticated and intelligent recommendation systems that can anticipate our needs, understand our preferences, and help us discover new and exciting things. This will transform how we consume information, make choices, and interact with the world around us.

5.4 Text Summarization and Generation

Alright, let's talk about how graph-powered LLMs can help us make sense of all the information overload we face every day. Think about the sheer volume of text we encounter – news articles, social media posts, emails, reports, and so on. It can be overwhelming to keep up with it all!

That's where text summarization comes in. It's the art of condensing information into a shorter, more manageable form while preserving the key ideas and meaning. And graph-powered LLMs are taking text summarization to a whole new level, making it more accurate, informative, and personalized.

But that's not all! These powerful models can also generate new text based on the information in a knowledge graph, opening up exciting possibilities for creative content generation and knowledge exploration.

How Knowledge Graphs Enhance Summarization

By incorporating knowledge graphs into text summarization, we can:

1. Identify Key Information: Knowledge graphs can help LLMs identify the most important entities, relationships, and events in a document, allowing them to focus on summarizing the most relevant information. This avoids generating summaries that are too general or miss out on crucial details.

2. Generate Concise and Informative Summaries: LLMs can leverage the knowledge graph to generate summaries that are both concise and informative, capturing the essence of the document without unnecessary details. This makes it easier for people to quickly grasp the main points of a long text.

3. Provide Different Levels of Detail: Depending on the user's needs, LLMs can generate summaries at different levels of detail. They can provide a high-level overview, focus on specific aspects of the document, or even generate summaries tailored to different audiences.

4. Personalize Summaries: By accessing user information and preferences stored in the knowledge graph, LLMs can generate summaries that are personalized to each user's interests and needs. This makes the summaries more relevant and engaging.

Real-World Examples

This enhanced summarization capability has significant implications for various applications:

- News and media: LLMs can be used to generate summaries of news articles, making it easier for people to stay informed about current events.

- Scientific literature: Researchers can use LLMs to quickly understand the key findings of scientific papers, saving them time and effort.
- Business intelligence: LLMs can summarize reports and presentations, providing executives with a quick overview of important information.
- Education: Students can use LLMs to summarize textbooks and lecture notes, making it easier to study and learn.

How Knowledge Graphs Enable Text Generation

Beyond summarization, graph-powered LLMs can also generate new text based on the information in a knowledge graph. This opens up exciting possibilities for:

- Creative content generation: LLMs can generate stories, poems, and articles based on the information and relationships in the knowledge graph. This can be used to create new forms of entertainment, educational content, or even personalized marketing materials.
- Knowledge exploration: LLMs can generate different perspectives on a topic by exploring different paths and connections in the knowledge graph. This can help users discover new information and gain a deeper understanding of a subject.
- Personalized content creation: LLMs can generate personalized content based on user information and preferences stored in the knowledge graph. This can be used to create customized news feeds, product recommendations, or even personalized stories.

Real-World Examples

This text generation capability has various applications:

- Marketing and advertising: LLMs can generate personalized marketing copy and product descriptions based on customer data and product information in a knowledge graph.

- Social media content creation: LLMs can generate engaging social media posts based on current events, trending topics, and user interests.
- Creative writing: LLMs can assist writers by generating ideas, characters, and plot points based on information in a knowledge graph.

Example

Let's say you want to generate a biography of a historical figure. You could use a graph-powered LLM to access information about the person's life, achievements, and relationships from a knowledge graph. The LLM could then generate a comprehensive and engaging biography, highlighting key events, accomplishments, and connections to other important figures.

Code Example

Python

```python
# Sample knowledge graph (replace with your
actual knowledge graph)

knowledge_graph = {

    "Albert Einstein": {

        "born": "1879",

        "died": "1955",
```

```python
        "occupation": "physicist",

        "known for": ["theory of relativity",
"E=mc²"],

    }

}


# Generate a simple biography from the knowledge
graph

entity = "Albert Einstein"

info = knowledge_graph[entity]

text = f"{entity} was a renowned
{info['occupation']} who lived from
{info['born']} to {info['died']}. He is best
known for his groundbreaking work on the
{info['known for']} and the famous equation
{info['known for']}."


# Print the generated text

print(text)
```

This code snippet demonstrates a simple way to generate text from a knowledge graph. You can adapt this code to your specific needs and knowledge graph structure.

The Future of Text Summarization and Generation

Graph-powered LLMs are transforming how we interact with text, making it easier to understand, summarize, and even generate new content. As the technology continues to evolve, we can expect even more sophisticated and powerful tools that can help us make sense of the information overload and unlock new forms of creative expression and knowledge discovery.

5.5 Knowledge Discovery and Data Analysis

Alright, let's explore how graph-powered LLMs can help us unlock the hidden knowledge and insights buried within massive amounts of data. Think of it like this: knowledge graphs are like vast treasure maps, filled with valuable information and connections, but sometimes it's hard to know where to start digging.[1]

That's where LLMs come in. With their ability to understand language, reason over complex relationships, and generate insightful summaries, they can act as our guides, helping us navigate the knowledge graph and uncover hidden gems.

How LLMs Enhance Knowledge Discovery

By combining LLMs with knowledge graphs, we can:

1. Identify Patterns and Trends: LLMs can analyze the connections and relationships in the knowledge graph to identify patterns and trends that might not be obvious to humans.[2] For example, they might discover that certain diseases are more prevalent in specific geographical areas or that certain products are frequently purchased together.

2. Uncover Hidden Connections: LLMs can use their reasoning abilities to uncover hidden connections and relationships between entities. This could involve finding unexpected links between different research areas, identifying potential collaborators based on shared interests, or even predicting future trends based on historical patterns.

3. Generate Hypotheses: LLMs can generate hypotheses based on the information in the knowledge graph, which can then be tested by human experts.[3] This can accelerate the research process and lead to new discoveries.

4. Explain Findings: LLMs can explain their findings in natural language, making it easier for humans to understand the insights and implications of the analysis.

Real-World Examples

This knowledge discovery capability has significant implications for various applications:

- Drug discovery: LLMs can analyze biological data and identify potential drug targets or drug interactions, accelerating the development of new treatments and cures.[4]
- Fraud detection: LLMs can analyze financial transactions and identify patterns that might indicate fraudulent activity, helping to prevent financial losses and protect consumers.[5]
- Social network analysis: LLMs can analyze social networks to identify influential individuals or communities, understand how information spreads, and even predict social trends.[6]
- Customer relationship management: LLMs can analyze customer data to identify customer segments, predict churn, and personalize marketing campaigns.[7]

Example

Let's say you're a researcher interested in understanding the latest trends in artificial intelligence. You could use a graph-powered LLM to analyze a knowledge graph of research publications, identifying emerging topics, influential researchers, and connections between different research areas. This could help you stay up-to-date with the latest advancements and identify promising areas for future research.

Code Example

Python

```python
import networkx as nx



# Sample knowledge graph (replace with your
actual knowledge graph)

graph = nx.Graph()

graph.add_edges_from([

    ("Artificial Intelligence", "Machine
Learning", {"label": "subfield"}),

    ("Machine Learning", "Deep Learning",
{"label": "subfield"}),

    ("Deep Learning", "Computer Vision",
{"label": "application"}),
```

```python
    ("Deep Learning", "Natural Language
Processing", {"label": "application"}),

])
```

```python
# Find related concepts to "Artificial
Intelligence"

related_concepts = nx.ego_graph(graph,
"Artificial Intelligence", radius=2)
```

```python
# Print the related concepts

print("Related concepts to Artificial
Intelligence:")

for node in related_concepts.nodes:

    print(node)
```

This code snippet demonstrates how to use the NetworkX library in Python to find related concepts to a given entity in a knowledge graph. This can be used to explore connections between different concepts and identify potential areas for further investigation.

The Future of Knowledge Discovery

Graph-powered LLMs are transforming how we discover and analyze knowledge, making it easier to extract insights, uncover hidden connections, and generate new hypotheses.[8] As the technology continues to evolve, we can expect even more powerful tools that can help us make sense of complex data, accelerate scientific discovery, and solve real-world problems. This will unlock new possibilities for innovation and progress across various fields, from healthcare and education to business and technology.[9]

5.6 Other Applications

The applications of graph-powered LLMs are truly vast and continue to expand as the technology evolves. We've already explored some of the key areas where they're making a significant impact, but let's take a look at a few more examples that showcase the versatility and potential of this powerful combination.

1. Code Generation: From Natural Language to Software

Imagine describing what you want a program to do in plain English, and then having an AI system generate the actual code for you. That's the promise of code generation using graph-powered LLMs.

By combining the language understanding capabilities of LLMs with the structured knowledge of code repositories and programming languages represented in knowledge graphs, we can create systems that:

- Translate natural language into code: You could describe a task like "create a function that calculates the average of a list of numbers" and the LLM, guided by the knowledge graph, would generate the corresponding Python code.
- Generate code snippets and templates: LLMs can generate code snippets or templates for common programming tasks, saving developers time and effort.

- Assist with debugging and code completion: LLMs can analyze code, identify potential errors, and suggest fixes or completions, making the coding process more efficient.

This has the potential to democratize software development, making it easier for people without coding experience to create simple programs and automate tasks. It can also help experienced developers write code faster and with fewer errors.

Real-world examples

- GitHub Copilot: This AI-powered code completion tool uses a massive code repository and an LLM to suggest code completions and generate entire functions based on natural language descriptions.
- Tabnine: Another code completion tool that uses LLMs and knowledge graphs to provide intelligent suggestions and improve developer productivity.

2. Machine Translation: Breaking Down Language Barriers

LLMs have already made significant strides in machine translation, but graph-powered LLMs can take it even further. By incorporating knowledge graphs that capture the nuances of different languages, cultural contexts, and domain-specific terminology, we can create translation systems that are:

- More accurate: LLMs can use the knowledge graph to disambiguate words and phrases, ensuring that the translation is faithful to the original meaning.
- More fluent: LLMs can generate more natural and fluent translations by leveraging the knowledge graph to understand the grammatical structures and idiomatic expressions of different languages.
- More adaptable: LLMs can adapt to different domains and contexts, providing more accurate translations for specialized fields like medicine, law, or finance.

This can help break down language barriers and facilitate communication and understanding across cultures.

Real-world examples

- Google Translate: Google Translate is already using knowledge graphs to improve the accuracy and fluency of its translations.
- Microsoft Translator: Microsoft Translator also uses knowledge graphs to enhance its translation capabilities, particularly for specific domains like healthcare and finance.

3. Sentiment Analysis: Understanding Emotions and Opinions

LLMs can be used to analyze text and identify the sentiment expressed, such as positive, negative, or neutral. This is known as sentiment analysis, and it has various applications in social media monitoring, customer feedback analysis, and market research.

Graph-powered LLMs can enhance sentiment analysis by

- Considering context: They can use the knowledge graph to understand the context of the text, such as the relationship between the author and the subject, the tone of the conversation, and the cultural background. This can help them more accurately identify the sentiment expressed.
- Identifying nuanced emotions: They can go beyond simple positive/negative classifications and identify more nuanced emotions, such as joy, sadness, anger, or fear.
- Explaining sentiment: They can provide explanations for their sentiment analysis, highlighting the words and phrases that contributed to their assessment.

This can help businesses and organizations better understand their customers, track public opinion, and make more informed decisions.

Real-world examples

- Brandwatch: This social listening platform uses LLMs and knowledge graphs to analyze social media conversations and identify customer sentiment towards brands and products.
- Lexalytics: This text analytics platform uses LLMs and knowledge graphs to analyze customer feedback and identify key themes and sentiments.

The Expanding Horizon of Graph-Powered LLMs

These are just a few examples of the many exciting applications of graph-powered LLMs. As the technology continues to evolve, we can expect even more innovative and impactful uses to emerge, transforming various aspects of our lives and shaping the future of AI.

Chapter 6: Case Studies

We've talked a lot about the potential of graph-powered LLMs, but now let's dive into some specific case studies that showcase how this technology is actually being used to solve problems and create value across different industries.

6.1 Implementing Graph RAG for a Customer Service Chatbot

Alright, let's roll up our sleeves and get practical! We've talked about the potential of graph-powered LLMs, and now we're going to see how this technology can be used to build a truly helpful and efficient customer service chatbot.

Imagine you're running a busy online store that sells everything from electronics to clothing. You receive hundreds, maybe even thousands, of customer inquiries every day. People have questions about products, orders, shipping, returns, and more. It's a lot to handle, and providing timely and accurate support can be a real challenge.

This is where a graph-powered LLM can be a game-changer. By implementing a customer service chatbot that leverages Graph RAG, you can automate a significant portion of your customer interactions, freeing up your human agents to focus on more complex issues and ultimately improving customer satisfaction.

Building the Knowledge Graph

The first step is to build a comprehensive knowledge graph that captures all the essential information about your business and its operations. This knowledge graph will be the brain of your chatbot, providing it with the knowledge it needs to understand customer requests and provide accurate and helpful responses.

Here's what you might include in your knowledge graph

- Products: Detailed information about each product, including its features, specifications, price, availability, and customer reviews.
- Orders: Information about the order process, including order status, shipping information, and tracking details.
- Shipping: Details about shipping options, costs, delivery times, and potential delays.
- Returns: Information about the return policy, how to initiate a return, and refund processing.
- Troubleshooting: Troubleshooting guides for common issues, FAQs, and solutions to frequently encountered problems.
- Company policies: Information about your company's policies, such as privacy policy, terms of service, and customer support guidelines.

This knowledge graph should be structured in a way that's easy for the LLM to understand and navigate. It should also be constantly updated to reflect any changes in your products, services, or policies.

Training the LLM

Next, you need to train an LLM specifically for customer service conversations. This involves feeding it a massive dataset of customer service interactions, such as chat logs, emails, and transcripts of phone calls. The LLM will learn to:

- Understand customer requests: Identify the customer's intent, even if it's expressed in different ways.
- Extract relevant information: Identify the key entities and relationships in the customer's request, such as the product they're asking about or the order number they're referencing.

- Generate appropriate responses: Generate natural and helpful responses that address the customer's needs and provide relevant information.

Integrating with the Chatbot Interface

Once you have your knowledge graph and trained LLM, you need to integrate them with a chatbot interface. This could be a simple chat window on your website, a messaging app integration, or even a voice-activated assistant.

The chatbot interface should be user-friendly and intuitive, allowing customers to easily interact with the LLM and get the information they need.

Leveraging Graph RAG

Now, here's where the magic of Graph RAG comes in. When a customer interacts with the chatbot, the LLM uses graph retrieval techniques to access relevant information from the knowledge graph and generate personalized and accurate responses.

For example, if a customer asks, "What's the status of my order?", the LLM would

1. Identify the intent: Understand that the customer is asking about their order status.
2. Extract relevant entities: Identify the customer and their order number (if provided).
3. Retrieve information from the knowledge graph: Access the order information in the knowledge graph, including the current status, shipping details, and estimated delivery date.
4. Generate a response: Generate a natural language response that provides the customer with the requested information.

Benefits of a Graph-Powered Customer Service Chatbot

Implementing a graph-powered customer service chatbot can bring significant benefits to your business:

- Improved customer satisfaction: Customers get faster and more accurate answers to their questions, leading to higher satisfaction.
- Reduced costs: Automating customer service interactions can significantly reduce costs associated with human agents.
- Increased efficiency: The chatbot can handle a large volume of inquiries simultaneously, improving efficiency and reducing wait times.
- Personalized support: The chatbot can access customer data and preferences to provide personalized support and recommendations.
- 24/7 availability: The chatbot can provide support around the clock, even outside of normal business hours.

Code Example

Python

```python
# Sample knowledge graph (replace with your
actual knowledge graph)

knowledge_graph = {

    "orders": {

        "12345": {"status": "shipped",
"shipping_address": "123 Main St"},
```

```
        "67890": {"status": "processing",
"shipping_address": "456 Oak Ave"},

    }

}
```

User query

```
user_query = "What's the status of my order
12345?"
```

Extract the order number

```
order_number = user_query.split("order
").rstrip("?")
```

Retrieve order status from the knowledge graph

```
order_status =
knowledge_graph["orders"].get(order_number,
{}).get("status")
```

```python
# Generate a response

if order_status:

    response = f"The status of your order
{order_number} is {order_status}."

else:

    response = "I couldn't find an order with
that number. Please double-check the order number
and try again."


# Print the response

print(response)
```

This code snippet demonstrates a simple way to build a customer service chatbot using a knowledge graph. You can adapt this code to your specific needs and knowledge graph structure.

The Future of Customer Service

Graph-powered LLMs are transforming the customer service landscape, making it more efficient, personalized, and accessible. As the technology continues to evolve, we can expect even more sophisticated and intelligent chatbots that can understand complex requests, provide proactive support, and even anticipate customer needs. This will lead to a future where customer service is seamless, effortless, and truly customer-centric.

6.2 Using Graph RAG for Medical Diagnosis

The field of medicine is ripe for disruption by AI, and graph-powered LLMs are poised to play a crucial role in this transformation. Imagine a world where doctors have access to an AI assistant that can analyze patient symptoms, medical history, and the latest research to provide diagnostic suggestions and treatment recommendations. This isn't science fiction; it's becoming a reality thanks to Graph RAG.

Let's explore how this technology can be applied to medical diagnosis, potentially revolutionizing healthcare as we know it.

Building the Medical Knowledge Graph

The first step is to construct a comprehensive medical knowledge graph. This is no small feat! It needs to encompass a vast amount of information, including:

- Diseases: Detailed information about various diseases, including their symptoms, causes, risk factors, diagnostic criteria, and treatment options.
- Symptoms: A comprehensive list of symptoms, their possible causes, and their relationships to different diseases.
- Treatments: Information about various treatments, including medications, surgical procedures, therapies, and their effectiveness for different conditions.
- Drugs: Detailed information about drugs, including their mechanisms of action, side effects, interactions with other drugs, and dosage recommendations.
- Medical procedures: Information about medical procedures, their risks and benefits, and their suitability for different patients.

- Medical literature: Links to relevant research papers, clinical trials, and medical guidelines, providing the latest evidence and best practices.

This medical knowledge graph needs to be meticulously curated, ensuring accuracy and reliability. It also needs to be constantly updated with the latest medical research and clinical findings.

Training the LLM

Next, we need to train an LLM specifically for medical applications. This involves feeding it a massive dataset of:

- Electronic health records (EHRs): Real-world patient data, including symptoms, diagnoses, treatments, and outcomes.
- Clinical trials: Data from clinical trials, including patient demographics, treatment protocols, and results.
- Medical literature: A vast corpus of medical research papers, textbooks, and clinical guidelines.

By learning from this data, the LLM can develop a deep understanding of medical terminology, disease processes, and treatment options. It can also learn to identify patterns and make connections that might not be obvious to human doctors.

Integrating with the Diagnostic System

Once the medical knowledge graph and the LLM are ready, they need to be integrated with a user-friendly diagnostic system. This system could be a web application, a mobile app, or even integrated into existing electronic health record systems.

Doctors would then be able to use this system to

- Input patient information: Enter patient symptoms, medical history, and test results.

- Receive diagnostic suggestions: The LLM would analyze the patient information and generate a list of possible diagnoses, ranked by their likelihood.
- Explore treatment options: The LLM would provide information about potential treatment options for each diagnosis, including their effectiveness, risks, and benefits.
- Access supporting evidence: The LLM would provide links to relevant research papers and clinical guidelines to support its diagnostic suggestions and treatment recommendations.

Leveraging Graph RAG

The key to this system's power lies in Graph RAG. When a doctor inputs patient information, the LLM uses graph retrieval techniques to access relevant information from the medical knowledge graph and generate diagnostic hypotheses and treatment options.

For example, if a patient presents with symptoms of fever, cough, and shortness of breath, the LLM would:

1. Identify potential diseases: Use the knowledge graph to identify diseases associated with these symptoms, such as pneumonia, influenza, or COVID-19.
2. Consider patient history: Access the patient's medical history from the EHR to identify any pre-existing conditions or risk factors that might influence the diagnosis.
3. Analyze risk factors: Use the knowledge graph to assess the patient's risk factors for each potential disease, such as age, smoking history, or exposure to infectious agents.
4. Generate diagnostic suggestions: Rank the potential diagnoses based on their likelihood, considering the patient's symptoms, medical history, and risk factors.
5. Recommend treatment options: Provide information about potential treatment options for each diagnosis, taking into

account the patient's individual circumstances and preferences.

Benefits of Graph RAG in Medical Diagnosis

Using Graph RAG for medical diagnosis can bring significant benefits to healthcare:

- Improved diagnostic accuracy: LLMs can consider a vast amount of medical knowledge and identify potential diagnoses that a human doctor might miss.
- Personalized treatment: LLMs can tailor treatment recommendations to the individual patient, considering their medical history, allergies, and other factors.
- Reduced diagnostic errors: LLMs can help reduce diagnostic errors by providing doctors with a second opinion and supporting evidence.
- Accelerated research: LLMs can assist researchers in analyzing medical data and identifying potential new treatments or cures.
- Improved patient outcomes: By improving diagnostic accuracy and personalizing treatment, graph-powered LLMs can ultimately lead to better patient outcomes.

The Future of Medicine with Graph-Powered LLMs

Graph-powered LLMs have the potential to revolutionize healthcare, making it more accurate, efficient, and personalized. As the technology continues to evolve, we can expect even more sophisticated and intelligent systems that can assist doctors in diagnosis, treatment planning, and patient care. This will lead to a future where healthcare is more proactive, preventive, and ultimately more effective in improving human health and well-being.

6.3 Building a Knowledge-Intensive Question Answering System

Alright, let's explore how to build a question answering system that can tackle those really tough questions, the ones that require deep knowledge and reasoning. Think about questions like:

- "What were the long-term effects of colonialism on Nigerian society?"
- "How does climate change impact food security in Africa?"
- "What are the ethical implications of artificial intelligence?"

These aren't the kind of questions you can just Google and get a simple answer. They require understanding complex concepts, connecting different pieces of information, and even drawing inferences and conclusions.

This is where graph-powered LLMs shine. By combining the language understanding of LLMs with the rich knowledge and connections in a knowledge graph, we can build question answering systems that can tackle these challenging questions and provide insightful and comprehensive answers.

Building a Comprehensive Knowledge Graph

The first step, as always, is to build a solid foundation of knowledge. In this case, that means creating a comprehensive knowledge graph that covers a wide range of topics and domains. This could include:

- History: Events, people, places, and their relationships throughout history.
- Science: Scientific concepts, theories, discoveries, and their interconnections.
- Literature: Authors, books, characters, themes, and literary movements.

- Geography: Countries, cities, landmarks, and their geographical relationships.
- Current events: Up-to-date information about news, politics, and world affairs.
- Domain-specific knowledge: Specialized knowledge in areas like medicine, law, finance, or technology.

The more comprehensive the knowledge graph, the more questions the system will be able to answer. It's also crucial to ensure that the knowledge graph is well-structured, with clear relationships and connections between entities.

Training a Knowledge-Aware LLM

Next, we need to train an LLM that can effectively utilize this knowledge graph.

This involves:

- Training on a massive dataset: The LLM should be trained on a vast corpus of text and code, including books, articles, websites, and code repositories. This will give it a broad understanding of language and concepts.
- Incorporating the knowledge graph: The LLM should be trained on the knowledge graph itself, learning to understand its structure, relationships, and entities. This will enable it to navigate the graph and retrieve relevant information.
- Teaching it to reason: The LLM should be trained on question-answer pairs, learning to understand different types of questions, extract relevant information from the knowledge graph, and generate comprehensive and informative answers.

Integrating with a Question Answering Interface

Once the knowledge graph and the LLM are ready, we need to integrate them with a user-friendly interface. This could be a web application, a mobile app, or even a voice-activated assistant.

The interface should allow users to

- Ask questions in natural language: Users should be able to ask questions in their own words, without having to use specific keywords or syntax.
- Receive comprehensive answers: The system should provide answers that are not just accurate but also comprehensive and informative, including relevant context, supporting evidence, and different perspectives.
- Explore related information: Users should be able to easily explore related information and concepts by clicking on links or asking follow-up questions.
- Personalize their experience: The system could allow users to personalize their experience by specifying their interests, knowledge level, or preferred learning style.

Leveraging Graph RAG

The key to this system's power lies in Graph RAG. When a user asks a question, the LLM uses graph retrieval techniques to access relevant information from the knowledge graph and generate a comprehensive answer.

For example, if a user asks, "What were the main causes of the Nigerian Civil War?", the LLM would

1. Understand the question: Analyze the question to identify the key entities and relationships involved, such as "Nigerian Civil War" and "causes."

2. Retrieve relevant information: Use graph retrieval techniques to find relevant information in the knowledge graph, such as the political tensions, economic disparities, and ethnic conflicts that led to the war.

3. Generate a comprehensive answer: Combine its language generation abilities with the retrieved knowledge to generate a comprehensive and informative answer, potentially including details about specific events, people, and their roles in the conflict.

Benefits of a Knowledge-Intensive Question Answering System

Building a knowledge-intensive question answering system can bring significant benefits:

- Access to deep knowledge: Users can get answers to complex questions that require deep knowledge and reasoning.
- Comprehensive and informative answers: The LLM can provide answers that are not just accurate but also comprehensive and informative, including relevant context and supporting evidence.
- Personalized learning: The system can be used for personalized learning, adapting to the user's knowledge level and providing explanations and examples tailored to their needs.
- Knowledge discovery: The system can be used for knowledge discovery, helping users explore connections between different concepts and uncover hidden insights.

Code Example

Python

```
# Sample knowledge graph (replace with your
actual knowledge graph)
```

```python
knowledge_graph = {

    "Nigerian Civil War": {

        "causes": [

            "political tensions",

            "economic disparities",

            "ethnic conflicts"

        ],

        "years": "1967-1970"

    }

}



# User question

user_question = "What were the main causes of the
Nigerian Civil War?"



# Extract the entity and relationship from the
question
```

```python
entity = "Nigerian Civil War"

relationship = "causes"


# Retrieve the answer from the knowledge graph

answer = knowledge_graph.get(entity,
{}).get(relationship)


# Generate a response

if answer:

    response = f"The main causes of the {entity}
were: {', '.join(answer)}."

else:

    response = "I couldn't find the answer to
your question."


# Print the response

print(response)
```

This code snippet demonstrates a simple way to build a knowledge-intensive question answering system using a knowledge graph. You can adapt this code to your specific needs and knowledge graph structure.

The Future of Question Answering

Graph-powered LLMs are paving the way for a new generation of question answering systems that can provide deeper, more comprehensive, and more personalized answers. As the technology continues to evolve, we can expect even more sophisticated and intelligent systems that can understand complex questions, reason over vast amounts of knowledge, and provide insights that were previously inaccessible. This will transform how we learn, make decisions, and interact with the world around us.

Chapter 7: Advanced Topics in Graph RAG

This chapter is for those who really want to push the boundaries of what's possible with this technology and explore the exciting research happening at the forefront of knowledge-enhanced LLMs.

7.1 Graph Construction and Knowledge Extraction

Okay, so we've spent a good amount of time exploring how to *use* knowledge graphs with LLMs. But what if the knowledge graph you need doesn't exist yet? What if you're working in a specialized field or tackling a unique problem that requires a custom-built knowledge base? That's where graph construction and knowledge extraction come into play.

Think of it like this: if you want a truly personalized house, you don't just buy one off the shelf; you work with an architect to design it from the ground up. Similarly, if you want a knowledge graph that perfectly fits your needs, you might need to build it yourself, carefully selecting the information and relationships that are relevant to your specific domain or task.

Graph Construction

Graph construction is the process of creating a new knowledge graph from scratch. It's like creating a blueprint for your knowledge, defining the structure, entities, and relationships that will form the foundation of your knowledge base.

This involves several key steps

1. Defining the Scope: First, you need to clearly define the scope of your knowledge graph. What topics and domains

will it cover? What kind of questions do you want it to be able to answer? What tasks do you want it to support?

2. Identifying Entities and Relationships: Next, you need to identify the key entities and relationships that are relevant to your domain. This might involve brainstorming with experts, analyzing existing data sources, or using natural language processing (NLP) techniques to extract entities and relationships from text.

3. Designing the Schema: Once you have a good understanding of the entities and relationships, you need to design the schema for your knowledge graph. This involves defining the types of entities and relationships, their attributes, and any constraints or rules that govern them.

4. Selecting a Storage Solution: You also need to decide how you're going to store and manage your knowledge graph. This might involve choosing a graph database, a triple store, or even a traditional relational database.

Knowledge Extraction

Once you have your blueprint, it's time to start populating your knowledge graph with actual data. This is where knowledge extraction comes in. It's the process of extracting knowledge from various sources and converting it into a structured format that can be used to build your knowledge graph.

Here are some common sources of knowledge

- Text documents: Books, articles, reports, web pages, and social media posts can all contain valuable information that can be extracted and added to the knowledge graph.
- Databases: Existing databases can be a rich source of structured information, such as customer data, product information, or financial records.
- APIs: You can use APIs to access real-time data from external sources, such as weather information, stock prices, or social media trends.

- Human expertise: Sometimes, the best source of knowledge is human experts who can provide insights and information that might not be readily available in other sources.

Extracting knowledge from these sources can be challenging. It often involves using NLP techniques to identify entities, relationships, and facts in text, as well as data cleaning and transformation techniques to ensure the quality and consistency of the extracted information.

Example

Let's say you're building a knowledge graph for Nigerian cuisine. You might

1. Define the scope: Focus on traditional Nigerian dishes, ingredients, cooking methods, and cultural significance.
2. Identify entities and relationships: Identify entities like "Egusi Soup," "Pounded Yam," "Palm Oil," and "Nigeria," and relationships like "is a dish," "is an ingredient in," and "is a region of."
3. Design the schema: Define attributes like "taste," "preparation time," and "region of origin" for dishes, and "nutritional value" and "source" for ingredients.
4. Extract knowledge: Extract information from cookbooks, online recipes, food blogs, and even interviews with Nigerian chefs.

Code Example

Python

```python
import spacy
```

```python
# Load the spaCy language model

nlp = spacy.load("en_core_web_sm")



# Sample text

text = "Egusi Soup is a popular Nigerian dish
made with ground melon seeds, leafy vegetables,
and palm oil."



# Process the text with spaCy

doc = nlp(text)



# Extract entities

entities = [(ent.text, ent.label_) for ent in
doc.ents]



# Print the entities

print(entities)  # Output: [('Egusi Soup',
'WORK_OF_ART'), ('Nigerian', 'NORP')]
```

This code snippet demonstrates how to use the spaCy library in Python to extract entities from text. You can adapt this code to your specific needs and knowledge extraction task.

The Importance of Custom Knowledge Graphs

Building custom knowledge graphs can be a valuable investment for organizations and researchers who need a knowledge base that's tailored to their specific needs. By carefully designing the graph and extracting relevant knowledge, you can create a powerful tool for enhancing LLMs and enabling new applications.

7.2 Reasoning and Inference over Knowledge Graphs

Okay, so we've built our knowledge graph, this amazing network of interconnected information. But now what? How do we actually *use* it to gain insights, answer complex questions, and make informed decisions? That's where reasoning and inference come in.

Think of it like this: a knowledge graph is like a map of a city, showing you all the streets, buildings, and landmarks. But to truly understand the city, you need to be able to navigate that map, find your way around, and discover hidden connections. Reasoning and inference are like your navigation tools, allowing you to explore the knowledge graph and uncover its hidden treasures.

What is Reasoning and Inference?

In the context of knowledge graphs, reasoning and inference refer to the process of using logical rules and algorithms to derive new knowledge or insights from the existing information in the graph. It's like playing detective, using the clues in the knowledge graph to piece together a complete picture.

Here are some common types of reasoning and inference

- Deductive reasoning: This involves drawing conclusions based on established rules and facts. For example, if the knowledge graph states that "all birds have feathers" and that "a penguin is a bird," you can deduce that "a penguin has feathers."
- Inductive reasoning: This involves drawing general conclusions based on specific observations or examples. For example, if the knowledge graph contains many examples of Nigerian authors who have won literary awards, you might infer that Nigerian literature is highly acclaimed.
- Abductive reasoning: This involves finding the best explanation for a set of observations. For example, if a patient presents with symptoms of fever, cough, and fatigue, the knowledge graph can be used to infer the most likely diagnosis based on the known causes of these symptoms.

Why is Reasoning Important?

Reasoning and inference allow us to go beyond simply retrieving information from the knowledge graph. They enable us to:

- Discover new knowledge: By connecting the dots between different pieces of information, we can uncover hidden relationships and insights that were not explicitly stated in the knowledge graph.
- Answer complex questions: We can answer questions that require understanding multiple relationships and drawing inferences, such as "What were the long-term consequences of the Nigerian Civil War?" or "How does climate change impact food security in Africa?"
- Make informed decisions: We can use reasoning to weigh different options, evaluate potential outcomes, and make informed decisions based on the available evidence and knowledge.

- Explain and justify conclusions: We can use reasoning to explain how we arrived at a particular conclusion, providing transparency and accountability.

How LLMs Use Reasoning

LLMs can be equipped with reasoning capabilities by:

- Incorporating logical rules: LLMs can be trained on logical rules and axioms, allowing them to perform deductive reasoning.
- Learning from examples: LLMs can learn to perform inductive and abductive reasoning by analyzing examples of how humans reason and make inferences.
- Using graph algorithms: LLMs can leverage graph algorithms, such as pathfinding or centrality analysis, to explore the knowledge graph and identify relevant connections.

Real-World Applications

Reasoning and inference over knowledge graphs have numerous applications:

- Medical diagnosis: LLMs can use reasoning to diagnose patients based on their symptoms, medical history, and the latest medical knowledge.
- Financial analysis: LLMs can use reasoning to analyze financial data, identify trends, and make investment recommendations.
- Legal research: LLMs can use reasoning to analyze legal documents, identify relevant precedents, and support legal arguments.
- Scientific discovery: LLMs can use reasoning to analyze scientific data, generate hypotheses, and accelerate the research process.

Example

Imagine a doctor using an LLM-powered diagnostic system. The doctor inputs the patient's symptoms and medical history, and the LLM uses reasoning over a medical knowledge graph to generate a list of possible diagnoses. For each diagnosis, the LLM also provides a list of potential treatment options, along with their associated risks and benefits. The doctor can then use this information to make an informed decision about the best course of treatment for the patient.

Code Example

Python

```python
import networkx as nx

# Sample knowledge graph (replace with your
actual knowledge graph)

graph = nx.DiGraph()

graph.add_edges_from([

    ("fever", "influenza"),

    ("cough", "influenza"),

    ("influenza", "rest"),

    ("influenza", "antiviral medication")

])
```

```python
# Patient symptoms

symptoms = ["fever", "cough"]


# Find potential diagnoses

diagnoses =

for symptom in symptoms:

    for diagnosis in graph.successors(symptom):

        diagnoses.append(diagnosis)


# Find treatment options for the most likely
diagnosis

most_likely_diagnosis = max(set(diagnoses),
key=diagnoses.count)

treatment_options =
list(graph.successors(most_likely_diagnosis))
```

```
# Print the results

print(f"Most likely diagnosis:
{most_likely_diagnosis}")

print("Treatment options:")

for option in treatment_options:

    print(option)
```

This code snippet demonstrates how to use the NetworkX library in Python to perform pathfinding in a knowledge graph. In this example, the code finds potential diagnoses based on patient symptoms and then identifies treatment options for the most likely diagnosis.

The Power of Reasoning in LLMs

Reasoning and inference are powerful tools that enable LLMs to go beyond simple information retrieval and engage in more complex cognitive tasks. By incorporating reasoning capabilities into LLMs, we can create AI systems that are more intelligent, insightful, and capable of solving real-world problems. This will unlock new possibilities for knowledge discovery, decision-making, and human-computer collaboration.

In the next section, we'll explore another advanced topic: integrating graph neural networks with LLMs, which allows LLMs to learn directly from the structure of the knowledge graph and generate even more sophisticated outputs.

7.3 Integrating Graph Neural Networks with LLMs

Alright, let's explore a truly fascinating area where the worlds of graph neural networks (GNNs) and LLMs collide! We've already seen how GNNs can be used for graph retrieval, but their integration with LLMs goes far beyond that. By combining the strengths of these two powerful technologies, we can create AI systems that are more knowledgeable, adaptable, and capable of tackling complex tasks.

Why Integrate GNNs with LLMs?

LLMs excel at processing and generating human language, but they can sometimes struggle with understanding the underlying relationships and dependencies between entities. GNNs, on the other hand, are specifically designed to learn from graph-structured data, capturing the complex connections and patterns that LLMs might miss.

By integrating GNNs with LLMs, we can

1. Enhance LLM Understanding: GNNs can provide LLMs with a deeper understanding of the knowledge graph, allowing them to capture complex relationships and dependencies that might not be apparent from simple text-based analysis. This can improve their ability to reason, answer questions, and generate more informed responses.

2. Generate Graph-Structured Outputs: LLMs can be trained to generate outputs that are not just text but also graph structures, such as knowledge graphs or concept maps. This can be useful for tasks like knowledge representation, summarization, and visualization.

3. Enable Graph-Based Reasoning: LLMs can leverage GNNs to perform reasoning and inference directly over the knowledge graph, enabling them to solve complex

problems, make predictions, and explain their decisions in a more transparent way.

How to Integrate GNNs with LLMs

There are various ways to integrate GNNs with LLMs, depending on the specific task and the desired outcome. Some common approaches include:

- GNNs as Encoders: GNNs can be used to encode the knowledge graph into a numerical representation that captures its structure and features. This representation can then be fed as input to an LLM, providing it with a richer understanding of the knowledge.
- GNNs as Decoders: LLMs can be trained to generate graph-structured outputs, using GNNs as decoders to transform the LLM's internal representation into a graph structure.
- Joint Training: GNNs and LLMs can be trained jointly, allowing them to learn from each other and improve their performance on specific tasks.

Real-World Examples

This integration of GNNs and LLMs has exciting implications for various applications:

- Drug Discovery: GNNs can be used to analyze molecular structures and predict their properties, while LLMs can analyze research papers and extract relevant information about drug targets and mechanisms. By combining these capabilities, we can develop AI systems that can accelerate the drug discovery process.
- Social Network Analysis: GNNs can analyze social network graphs to identify influential individuals or communities, while LLMs can analyze social media posts and extract information about user sentiment and opinions. This can be used to understand how information spreads, predict social

trends, and even identify potential influencers for marketing campaigns.

- Recommendation Systems: GNNs can analyze user-item interaction graphs to understand user preferences and recommend relevant items, while LLMs can analyze user reviews and provide personalized explanations for the recommendations. This can lead to more accurate, diverse, and explainable recommendations.

Example

Let's say you're working with a large collection of news articles about Nigerian politics. You could use an LLM to analyze these articles and extract information about politicians, political parties, events, and their relationships. Then, you could use a GNN to organize this information into a knowledge graph, capturing the complex connections and dependencies between these entities. This knowledge graph could then be used to answer questions about Nigerian politics, generate summaries of political events, or even predict future political trends.

Code Example

Python

```python
import torch

from torch_geometric.nn import GCNConv

from transformers import BertModel




# Define a GNN model
```

```python
class GCN(torch.nn.Module):

    #... (Implementation as before)



# Define an LLM model

class LLM(torch.nn.Module):

    def __init__(self):

        super().__init__()

        self.bert =
BertModel.from_pretrained('bert-base-uncased')

        #... (Add layers for specific task)



    def forward(self, input_ids):

        #... (Process input with BERT and other
layers)



# Create a sample graph and text data

#...
```

```
# Instantiate the GNN and LLM models

gnn_model = GCN()

llm_model = LLM()



# Define optimizers and loss functions

#...



# Joint training loop

for epoch in range(num_epochs):

    #... (Train GNN on graph data)

    #... (Train LLM on text data)

    #... (Combine GNN and LLM outputs for joint
loss)

    #... (Backpropagate and update parameters)
```

This code snippet demonstrates a basic framework for jointly training a GNN and an LLM using PyTorch Geometric and

Transformers. You can adapt this code to your specific task and models.

The Future of GNNs and LLMs

The integration of GNNs and LLMs is a rapidly evolving field with immense potential. As these technologies continue to advance, we can expect even more sophisticated and powerful AI systems that can learn, reason, and generate knowledge in ways that were previously unimaginable. This will unlock new possibilities for solving complex problems, creating innovative applications, and enhancing human-computer interaction.

7.4 Explainable Graph RAG

As we venture deeper into the world of graph-powered LLMs, it's crucial to address a key challenge: their lack of transparency. LLMs, especially the larger and more complex ones, can often feel like "black boxes." We feed them input, they produce impressive output, but the internal workings remain shrouded in mystery. This lack of explainability can be a major obstacle to trust and adoption, especially in critical applications where understanding the reasoning behind an AI's decisions is paramount.

Think about it this way: if a doctor uses an AI system to diagnose a patient, they need to understand *why* the AI arrived at that diagnosis. What evidence did it consider? What factors influenced its decision? Without this understanding, it's difficult to trust the AI's recommendations and make informed decisions about patient care.

That's where explainable Graph RAG comes in. It's all about making the decision-making process of graph-powered LLMs more transparent and understandable to humans. This involves developing techniques to:

Trace the Reasoning Path: When an LLM uses a knowledge graph to answer a question or generate a response, we want to be able to trace the path through the graph that led to that output. This path reveals the connections and relationships that the LLM used to arrive at its conclusion, providing valuable insights into its reasoning process.

1. Imagine asking an LLM, "Why is Lagos prone to flooding?" An explainable Graph RAG system might respond with: This explanation, grounded in the knowledge graph, makes the LLM's reasoning clear and transparent.
2. Highlight Relevant Evidence: We want to be able to highlight the specific pieces of evidence from the knowledge graph that were used to support the LLM's conclusions. This allows us to verify the accuracy of the information and understand the basis for the LLM's decision.
3. Generate Natural Language Explanations: We want LLMs to be able to explain their reasoning in natural language, making their decisions more understandable to humans. This involves translating the complex internal workings of the LLM into clear and concise explanations that humans can easily grasp.

Why Explainability Matters

Explainable Graph RAG is crucial for several reasons:

- Building Trust: When we understand how an AI system works, we're more likely to trust its decisions. This is especially important in critical applications like healthcare, finance, and law, where AI systems are increasingly being used to make important decisions.
- Debugging and Improving Models: Explainability can help us identify and correct errors in LLM reasoning, leading to more accurate and reliable systems.
- Ensuring Fairness and Accountability: Explainability can help us ensure that AI systems are not biased or

discriminatory, and that their decisions are fair and accountable.

- Facilitating Human-AI Collaboration: Explainability can help humans and AI systems work together more effectively, allowing humans to understand and guide the AI's decision-making process.

Techniques for Explainable Graph RAG

Researchers are developing various techniques to achieve explainable Graph RAG, including:

- Attention mechanisms: These mechanisms highlight the parts of the knowledge graph that the LLM is focusing on when generating its output, providing insights into its decision-making process.
- Provenance tracking: This involves tracking the origin of the information used by the LLM, allowing us to trace the reasoning path and identify supporting evidence.
- Rule extraction: This involves extracting logical rules from the LLM's decision-making process, making its reasoning more transparent.
- Natural language generation: This involves training LLMs to generate natural language explanations of their decisions, making them more understandable to humans.

The Future of Explainable AI

Explainable Graph RAG is an essential step towards building trustworthy and responsible AI systems. As the technology continues to evolve, we can expect even more sophisticated and effective techniques for explaining the decisions of graph-powered LLMs. This will pave the way for wider adoption of AI in critical applications and foster a more collaborative and transparent relationship between humans and AI.

Chapter 8: Challenges and Opportunities

We've come a long way on our journey exploring the fascinating world of graph-powered LLMs! We've seen how they can enhance LLM capabilities, overcome limitations, and enable a wide range of exciting applications. But as with any emerging technology, there are still challenges to overcome and opportunities to explore. In this chapter, we'll take a look at some of the key challenges and opportunities that lie ahead for graph-powered LLMs.

8.1 Scalability and Efficiency

Okay, let's get real about a challenge that often pops up when we're dealing with cutting-edge tech like graph-powered LLMs: scalability. Think of it like this: you've built a fantastic model that works great on a small knowledge graph, maybe about the size of a neighborhood. But what happens when you want to apply it to a knowledge graph the size of a whole city, or even a country? Things can start to get a bit creaky.

The same goes for graph-powered LLMs. As knowledge graphs grow larger and more complex, with millions or even billions of nodes and edges, performing graph retrieval and reasoning operations can become computationally expensive. This can lead to slower response times, increased memory usage, and even the need for specialized hardware.

Why Scalability Matters

Scalability is crucial for several reasons:

- Handling Real-World Data: Many real-world knowledge graphs are massive. Think about the knowledge graph that Google uses to power its search engine, or the knowledge graph that Facebook uses to understand its users' social connections. These graphs contain billions of nodes and edges, and any system that wants to use them effectively needs to be able to handle that scale.

- Enabling Complex Applications: As we develop more sophisticated applications of graph-powered LLMs, such as question answering systems that can reason over vast amounts of knowledge or conversational AI agents that can maintain context over long interactions, scalability becomes even more important.
- Democratizing Access: If we want graph-powered LLMs to be accessible to a wide range of users and developers, we need to make them scalable and efficient, even on less powerful hardware.

Challenges to Scalability

Several factors contribute to the scalability challenges of graph-powered LLMs:

- Graph Traversal: Many graph algorithms, such as pathfinding or centrality analysis, involve traversing the graph, which can be time-consuming for large graphs.
- Graph Neural Networks: GNNs, while powerful, can also be computationally expensive, especially for large and complex graphs.
- Data Storage and Retrieval: Storing and retrieving large knowledge graphs efficiently can be a challenge, especially when dealing with distributed data or complex queries.
- LLM Inference: The inference process of LLMs, where they generate responses based on input and knowledge, can also be computationally expensive, especially for large and complex models.

Strategies for Achieving Scalability

Researchers are actively developing strategies to address these challenges and make graph-powered LLMs more scalable:

- Efficient Graph Algorithms: Developing more efficient algorithms for graph traversal, retrieval, and reasoning. This might involve using approximation techniques, parallel processing, or specialized data structures.
- Distributed Graph Processing: Distributing the workload across multiple machines to handle large knowledge graphs. This involves breaking down the graph into smaller chunks and processing them in parallel.
- Optimized Data Storage: Using optimized data structures and storage formats to efficiently store and retrieve large knowledge graphs. This might involve using graph databases, distributed file systems, or specialized indexing techniques.
- Model Compression: Compressing LLM models to reduce their size and computational requirements without significantly sacrificing performance. This can involve techniques like pruning, quantization, or knowledge distillation.
- Hardware Acceleration: Leveraging specialized hardware, such as GPUs or graph processing units, to accelerate graph computations and LLM inference.

Efficiency Matters Too

In addition to scalability, efficiency is also crucial for graph-powered LLMs. Even if a system can handle large knowledge graphs, it needs to be able to do so in a timely manner. This is especially important for applications that require real-time responses, such as conversational AI or question answering systems.

Strategies for improving efficiency include

- Caching: Storing frequently accessed information in a cache to avoid redundant computations.
- Indexing: Creating indexes for the knowledge graph to speed up retrieval.

- Query Optimization: Optimizing queries to reduce the amount of data that needs to be processed.

The Path to Scalable and Efficient Graph-Powered LLMs

Achieving scalability and efficiency in graph-powered LLMs is an ongoing challenge, but researchers are making significant progress. By combining efficient algorithms, distributed processing, optimized data storage, and hardware acceleration, we can build systems that can handle massive knowledge graphs and provide real-time responses. This will pave the way for even more sophisticated and impactful applications of graph-powered LLMs, transforming how we interact with information and solve complex problems.

8.2 Data Quality and Bias

Alright, let's have a serious chat about a crucial aspect of building any AI system, especially those that rely on knowledge graphs: data quality and bias. Think of it like baking a cake. If you use spoiled ingredients or the wrong measurements, your cake isn't going to turn out very well, right? The same goes for graph-powered LLMs. If the data in the knowledge graph is inaccurate, incomplete, or biased, the LLM's outputs will be too.

Why Data Quality Matters

Data quality is essential for several reasons:

- Accurate and Reliable Outputs: LLMs learn from the data they're fed. If the knowledge graph contains errors or inconsistencies, the LLM will learn those errors and produce inaccurate or unreliable outputs. This can have serious consequences in applications like medical diagnosis or financial analysis, where accuracy is paramount.
- Trustworthy AI: If users can't trust the information provided by an LLM, they're less likely to use it or rely on its

recommendations. Data quality is essential for building trust in AI systems and ensuring that they are used responsibly.

- Fair and Unbiased Decisions: Biased data can lead to biased outputs, perpetuating and even amplifying existing societal biases. This can have harmful consequences, especially in applications that affect people's lives, such as loan applications, hiring decisions, or criminal justice.

Sources of Data Quality Issues

Data quality issues can arise from various sources:

- Data Collection: Errors can occur during data collection, such as typos, missing values, or incorrect measurements.
- Data Integration: When combining data from different sources, inconsistencies and conflicts can arise due to different formats, naming conventions, or data quality standards.
- Human Bias: Human biases can creep into the data, either consciously or unconsciously, leading to skewed or unfair representations of reality.
- Data Decay: Data can become outdated or irrelevant over time, leading to inaccurate or misleading outputs.

Addressing Data Quality Issues

Ensuring data quality requires a multi-faceted approach:

- Data Cleaning: This involves identifying and correcting errors in the data, such as typos, missing values, or inconsistencies.
- Data Validation: This involves checking the data against predefined rules and constraints to ensure its accuracy and completeness.
- Data Transformation: This involves converting data from different sources into a common format and resolving any conflicts or inconsistencies.

- Data Enrichment: This involves adding additional information to the data, such as contextual information or metadata, to improve its quality and usefulness.

The Challenge of Bias

Bias in data is a particularly challenging issue, as it can be subtle and difficult to detect. Bias can manifest in various ways:

- Representation Bias: Certain groups or individuals might be underrepresented or overrepresented in the data, leading to skewed results.
- Measurement Bias: The way data is collected or measured can introduce bias, such as using biased survey questions or relying on data that is not representative of the population.
- Algorithmic Bias: The algorithms used to process and analyze data can also introduce bias, even if the data itself is unbiased.

Mitigating Bias

Mitigating bias requires a combination of technical and social approaches:

- Diverse Data: Ensuring that the data used to train LLMs and build knowledge graphs is diverse and representative of different groups and perspectives.
- Bias Detection: Developing techniques to detect and quantify bias in data and LLMs.
- Bias Mitigation: Developing algorithms and techniques to mitigate bias in LLMs and their outputs.
- Ethical Frameworks: Establishing ethical frameworks and guidelines for the development and use of graph-powered LLMs, ensuring that they are used fairly and responsibly.

The Importance of Ongoing Vigilance:

Ensuring data quality and mitigating bias is an ongoing process that requires constant vigilance and attention. It's not a one-time fix, but a continuous effort to improve the accuracy, fairness, and reliability of AI systems.

By addressing these challenges, we can build graph-powered LLMs that are not only intelligent but also trustworthy, ethical, and beneficial to society.

8.3 Ethical Considerations

As we continue to push the boundaries of AI and develop increasingly powerful technologies like graph-powered LLMs, it's crucial to step back and consider the ethical implications of our creations. These aren't just technical challenges; they're societal challenges that require careful thought, open discussion, and responsible action.

Why Ethics Matter in AI

AI systems are becoming increasingly integrated into our lives, influencing our decisions, shaping our perceptions, and even impacting our well-being. It's essential to ensure that these systems are developed and used in a way that aligns with our values and promotes a just and equitable society.

Ethical considerations in AI are particularly important because:

- AI systems can perpetuate and amplify existing biases: If the data used to train an AI system is biased, the system's outputs will be biased as well. This can lead to discrimination, unfair treatment, and even harm to individuals or groups.

- AI systems can be used to manipulate and deceive: AI systems can be used to create convincing fake videos, generate misleading news articles, or even impersonate real people. This can have serious consequences for individuals, organizations, and society as a whole.
- AI systems can have unintended consequences: Even with the best intentions, AI systems can have unintended consequences that can be harmful or even dangerous. It's crucial to anticipate and mitigate these risks.
- AI systems raise questions about responsibility and accountability: When an AI system makes a mistake or causes harm, who is responsible? How do we ensure accountability for AI decisions?

Key Ethical Considerations for Graph-Powered LLMs

Let's explore some of the key ethical considerations specific to graph-powered LLMs:

- Privacy: Knowledge graphs often contain personal data about individuals, such as their demographics, interests, relationships, and even medical history. It's crucial to ensure that this data is collected, stored, and used in a way that respects individual privacy and complies with data protection regulations.
- Fairness: As we discussed earlier, biased data can lead to biased outputs. It's essential to ensure that the knowledge graph and the LLM's training data are free from bias and that the system's outputs are fair and equitable to all individuals and groups.
- Transparency: The decision-making process of graph-powered LLMs can be complex and opaque. It's important to make this process more transparent and explainable to users, allowing them to understand how the system works and why it makes certain decisions.
- Accountability: When a graph-powered LLM makes a mistake or causes harm, it's important to have clear lines of

accountability. Who is responsible for the system's actions? How can we ensure that those responsible are held accountable?

- Misuse: Graph-powered LLMs can be misused for malicious purposes, such as generating fake news, spreading misinformation, or creating deepfakes. It's important to develop safeguards to prevent such misuse and ensure that the technology is used for good.

Addressing Ethical Challenges

Addressing these ethical challenges requires a multi-faceted approach:

- Ethical Frameworks: Developing ethical frameworks and guidelines for the development and use of graph-powered LLMs, drawing on insights from philosophy, ethics, and social sciences.
- Technical Solutions: Developing technical solutions to mitigate bias, enhance transparency, and ensure accountability in graph-powered LLMs.
- Regulation and Policy: Developing regulations and policies that govern the use of graph-powered LLMs, ensuring that they are used responsibly and ethically.
- Public Education: Educating the public about the capabilities and limitations of graph-powered LLMs, as well as the ethical considerations surrounding their use.

The Importance of Responsible AI

Developing and using graph-powered LLMs responsibly is not just a technical challenge; it's a societal challenge that requires collaboration between researchers, developers, policymakers, and the public. By addressing the ethical considerations proactively and thoughtfully, we can ensure that this powerful technology is used to benefit society and create a more just and equitable future.

8.4 Future Research Directions

The field of graph-powered LLMs is still relatively young, and there's a vast landscape of exciting research directions waiting to be explored. As we continue to push the boundaries of this technology, we can expect to see even more innovative and impactful applications that transform how we interact with information, make decisions, and solve problems.

Let's take a look at some of the key research areas that are likely to shape the future of graph-powered LLMs:

New GNN Architectures

Graph Neural Networks (GNNs) are the backbone of graph-powered LLMs, enabling them to learn from the structure and relationships in knowledge graphs. However, current GNN architectures have limitations in terms of expressiveness, efficiency, and scalability.

Future research in this area could focus on:

- Developing more expressive GNNs: Creating GNNs that can capture more complex and nuanced relationships in knowledge graphs, such as higher-order dependencies, temporal dynamics, and uncertainty.
- Improving GNN efficiency: Designing GNNs that are more computationally efficient, requiring less memory and processing power, especially for large and complex graphs.
- Enhancing GNN scalability: Developing GNNs that can scale to massive knowledge graphs with billions of nodes and edges, enabling applications in areas like social network analysis and web-scale knowledge representation.

Reasoning and Inference

While current graph-powered LLMs excel at retrieving information from knowledge graphs, they still have limitations when it comes to complex reasoning and inference. Future research could focus on:

- Developing more sophisticated reasoning algorithms: Creating algorithms that can handle different types of reasoning, such as deductive, inductive, and abductive reasoning, and can reason over complex and uncertain knowledge.
- Integrating symbolic and neural reasoning: Combining the strengths of symbolic AI, which excels at logical reasoning, with the learning capabilities of neural networks, to create more powerful and flexible reasoning systems.
- Reasoning with uncertainty: Developing methods for reasoning with uncertainty and incomplete knowledge, which is often the case in real-world applications.

Explainability and Interpretability

As graph-powered LLMs become more complex, it's crucial to make their decision-making process more transparent and understandable. Future research could focus on:

- Developing new explainability techniques: Creating new methods for tracing the reasoning path of LLMs, highlighting relevant evidence, and generating natural language explanations of their decisions.
- Evaluating explainability: Developing metrics and methods for evaluating the quality and effectiveness of explanations generated by LLMs.
- User-centered explainability: Designing explainability techniques that are tailored to the needs and understanding of different users, such as domain experts, decision-makers, or the general public.

Human-AI Collaboration

Graph-powered LLMs have the potential to be powerful partners for humans, assisting us in solving complex problems, making informed decisions, and gaining new insights. Future research could focus on:

- Developing interactive interfaces: Creating interfaces that allow humans to easily interact with graph-powered LLMs, ask questions, provide feedback, and guide their reasoning process.
- Human-in-the-loop learning: Developing methods for humans to provide feedback and guidance to LLMs, helping them learn and improve their performance over time.
- Collaborative problem-solving: Exploring how humans and graph-powered LLMs can work together to solve complex problems, leveraging the strengths of both human and artificial intelligence.

Applications in New Domains

Graph-powered LLMs have the potential to revolutionize various fields, from healthcare and education to finance and law. Future research could focus on:

- Developing domain-specific knowledge graphs: Creating knowledge graphs that are tailored to the specific needs and challenges of different domains.
- Adapting LLMs to new domains: Adapting LLMs to the specific language and knowledge requirements of different domains.
- Evaluating the impact of graph-powered LLMs: Evaluating the impact of graph-powered LLMs on different domains, assessing their effectiveness and identifying potential challenges and opportunities.

The Road Ahead

The future of graph-powered LLMs is filled with exciting possibilities. By continuing to invest in research and development, we can unlock the full potential of this technology and create AI systems that are more knowledgeable, capable, and trustworthy. This will lead to new discoveries, innovative applications, and a deeper understanding of the world around us.

Chapter 9: The Future of Knowledge and Intelligence

Now, it's time to take a step back and reflect on the broader implications of this technology. What does the future hold for graph-powered LLMs? How will they shape our understanding of knowledge and intelligence? And what impact will they have on society and industry?

9.1 The Role of Graph-Powered LLMs in the Future of AI

We've reached a pivotal moment in the evolution of artificial intelligence. While LLMs have shown remarkable abilities in generating human-quality text and engaging in seemingly intelligent conversations, they still face limitations when it comes to factual accuracy, reasoning, and understanding the complexities of the real world.[1] This is where graph-powered LLMs step in, offering a promising path towards a future where AI is not just intelligent but also deeply knowledgeable and contextually aware.

Think of it this way: LLMs are like gifted students who have mastered the art of language but lack the grounding in real-world knowledge and common sense.[2] Graph-powered LLMs, on the other hand, are like those same students who have also spent years studying encyclopedias, exploring maps, and conducting experiments. They possess both linguistic fluency and a deep understanding of how the world works.[3]

This combination of language processing and knowledge representation is poised to revolutionize the field of AI, enabling a wide range of applications that were previously out of reach.[4] Let's explore some of the key roles that graph-powered LLMs are likely to play in the future of AI:

1. Enhanced Natural Language Understanding

One of the most significant contributions of graph-powered LLMs is their potential to enhance natural language understanding (NLU). Traditional NLU systems often focus on analyzing the syntactic structure and individual words in a sentence, but they can struggle with understanding the nuances of meaning, context, and intent.

Graph-powered LLMs, by grounding language in a knowledge graph, can achieve a deeper level of understanding.[5]

They can:

- Resolve ambiguity: Using the knowledge graph to disambiguate words and phrases that have multiple meanings, ensuring that the AI understands the intended meaning in context.[6]
- Identify implicit relationships: Inferring relationships between entities that are not explicitly stated in the text, based on their connections in the knowledge graph.[7]
- Understand complex queries: Interpreting complex questions that involve multiple entities, relationships, and constraints, allowing for more accurate and comprehensive answers.[8]

This enhanced NLU capability will be crucial for building AI systems that can truly understand and respond to human language in a natural and meaningful way.

2. Knowledge Representation and Reasoning

Knowledge graphs provide a powerful way to represent and organize knowledge, capturing entities, relationships, and rules in a structured and machine-readable format.[9] Graph-powered LLMs can leverage this structured knowledge to:

- Reason over complex information: Using logical inference and graph algorithms to draw conclusions, make predictions, and solve problems based on the knowledge in the graph.[10]
- Integrate knowledge from multiple sources: Combining information from different sources, such as text documents, databases, and sensor data, to create a more comprehensive and holistic understanding of the world.[11]
- Adapt to new information: Updating and evolving their knowledge base as new information becomes available, ensuring that their responses and decisions are always based on the latest knowledge.[12]

This ability to represent, reason over, and adapt knowledge will be essential for building AI systems that can truly learn and evolve, becoming more intelligent and capable over time.

3. Human-AI Collaboration

Graph-powered LLMs can also play a crucial role in fostering more effective human-AI collaboration. By providing transparent and explainable outputs, grounded in a knowledge graph, these systems can:

- Build trust: Users can understand how the AI arrived at its conclusions, increasing their trust in its recommendations and decisions.[13]
- Facilitate communication: Humans and AI systems can communicate more effectively, sharing knowledge, asking questions, and providing feedback.[14]
- Support decision-making: AI systems can provide valuable insights and recommendations to humans, helping them make more informed decisions.[15]

This collaborative approach can lead to more effective problem-solving, innovation, and progress in various fields.

4. Explainable AI

As AI systems become more complex and integrated into our lives, it's increasingly important to ensure that their decisions are transparent and explainable. Graph-powered LLMs can contribute to this goal by:

- Providing traceable reasoning paths: Showing how the AI arrived at its conclusions by tracing the path through the knowledge graph that led to its output.[16]
- Highlighting relevant evidence: Identifying the specific pieces of evidence from the knowledge graph that were used to support the AI's decisions.
- Generating natural language explanations: Explaining the AI's reasoning in clear and concise natural language that humans can easily understand.

This explainability can help build trust in AI systems, ensure fairness and accountability, and facilitate human-AI collaboration.[17]

The Path Forward

Graph-powered LLMs are poised to play a transformative role in the future of AI, enabling more intelligent, knowledgeable, and context-aware systems that can truly understand and interact with the world around us. By continuing to research, develop, and deploy this technology responsibly, we can unlock its full potential and create a future where AI is not just a tool but a true partner in our quest for knowledge, understanding, and progress.

In the next section, we'll explore how graph-powered LLMs can help us build AI systems that are not just intelligent but also deeply knowledgeable and contextually aware.

9.2 Towards More Knowledgeable and Context-Aware AI Systems

One of the most exciting prospects of graph-powered LLMs is their potential to create AI systems that are not just intelligent but also truly knowledgeable and context-aware. These systems would be able to:

- Understand the world: They would have a deep understanding of the world, including its entities, relationships, and dynamics.
- Reason and make inferences: They would be able to reason and make inferences based on their knowledge, drawing conclusions and making predictions.
- Learn and adapt: They would be able to learn and adapt to new information and situations, continuously expanding their knowledge and improving their performance.
- Communicate effectively: They would be able to communicate effectively with humans, understanding their needs and providing relevant and informative responses.

This would enable AI systems to be more helpful, reliable, and trustworthy partners for humans, assisting us in various tasks and domains.

The Impact on Society and Industry

The widespread adoption of graph-powered LLMs has the potential to transform various aspects of society and industry:

- Education: Personalized learning experiences, intelligent tutoring systems, and automated essay grading.
- Healthcare: Improved medical diagnosis, personalized treatment plans, and drug discovery.
- Finance: Fraud detection, risk assessment, and investment analysis.

- Customer service: More efficient and personalized customer support.
- Law: Legal research, document analysis, and contract review.
- Journalism: Automated news summarization and fact-checking.

This is just a glimpse of the potential impact. As the technology continues to evolve, we can expect even more transformative applications to emerge, shaping the future of work, education, healthcare, and many other aspects of our lives.

The Future is Bright

The future of knowledge and intelligence is intertwined with the development and application of graph-powered LLMs. This technology has the potential to unlock new levels of understanding, enable more effective problem-solving, and foster a more collaborative relationship between humans and AI.

While there are challenges to overcome and ethical considerations to address, the future of graph-powered LLMs is bright. By continuing to research, develop, and deploy this technology responsibly, we can create a future where AI is not just intelligent but also knowledgeable, context-aware, and truly beneficial to society.

Thank you for joining me on this journey through the world of graph-powered LLMs. I hope this book has inspired you to explore this exciting field and contribute to its development and application. The future is full of possibilities, and I'm excited to see what we can achieve together.

9.3 The Impact on Society and Industry

We've explored the exciting capabilities of graph-powered LLMs and how they can enhance AI systems. Now, let's step back and consider the broader picture: how might this technology impact our society and the industries that shape our world?

The truth is, it's still early days, but the potential for transformation is immense. Graph-powered LLMs are not just about making AI smarter; they're about making AI more useful, more reliable, and more aligned with human needs and values. This has profound implications for how we live, work, and interact with technology.

Transforming Industries

Let's explore how graph-powered LLMs could revolutionize various industries:

Healthcare

Imagine a world where medical diagnoses are more accurate, treatment plans are personalized, and drug discovery is accelerated.[1] Graph-powered LLMs can analyze patient data, medical literature, and clinical trials to assist doctors in making informed decisions, leading to better patient outcomes and a healthier society.[2]

Example: A hospital could use a graph-powered LLM to analyze patient records and identify individuals at high risk of developing certain diseases, allowing for early intervention and preventive care.[3]

Education

Learning can become more personalized and engaging with AI tutors that adapt to individual student needs and provide tailored feedback.[4] Graph-powered LLMs can analyze student performance, identify knowledge gaps, and recommend relevant learning resources, creating a more effective and equitable education system.[5]

Example: An online learning platform could use a graph-powered LLM to create personalized learning paths for students, recommending courses and materials that match their interests and learning goals.[6]

Finance

Financial institutions can leverage graph-powered LLMs to detect fraud, assess risk, and make more informed investment decisions.[7] By analyzing financial data, market trends, and customer profiles, these systems can help protect consumers, improve financial stability, and drive economic growth.

Example: A bank could use a graph-powered LLM to analyze transaction patterns and identify potentially fraudulent activities, preventing financial losses and protecting customers.[8]

Customer Service

Say goodbye to frustrating interactions with automated customer service systems! Graph-powered LLMs can understand complex customer requests, access relevant information from knowledge bases, and provide personalized and helpful solutions, leading to increased customer satisfaction and loyalty.[9]

Example: A telecommunications company could use a graph-powered LLM to power its customer service chatbot, providing instant and accurate answers to customer questions about billing, plans, and technical support.[10]

Law

Legal professionals can use graph-powered LLMs to research case law, analyze legal documents, and identify relevant precedents, improving efficiency and accuracy in legal proceedings.[11] This can lead to a more just and equitable legal system.

Example: A law firm could use a graph-powered LLM to analyze contracts, identify potential risks and obligations, and ensure compliance with relevant regulations.[12]

Journalism and Media

Graph-powered LLMs can assist journalists in fact-checking information, generating summaries of news articles, and even creating personalized news feeds for readers.[13] This can lead to more informed and engaged citizens.

Example: A news organization could use a graph-powered LLM to automatically generate summaries of breaking news events, providing concise and accurate information to its audience.[14]

Shaping Society

Beyond specific industries, graph-powered LLMs have the potential to shape society in profound ways:

- Improved Decision-Making: By providing access to comprehensive knowledge and enabling more sophisticated reasoning, these systems can support better decision-making in various domains, from personal finance to public policy.[15]
- Enhanced Communication: They can facilitate more effective communication between people, breaking down language barriers and enabling more nuanced and understanding conversations.[16]
- Increased Accessibility: They can make information and knowledge more accessible to people, regardless of their background or expertise, empowering individuals and communities.[17]
- Accelerated Innovation: By connecting different ideas and uncovering hidden patterns, they can spark new discoveries and drive innovation across various fields.

The Challenges Ahead

While the potential benefits of graph-powered LLMs are immense, it's important to acknowledge the challenges that lie ahead:

- Ensuring Data Quality and Fairness: As we discussed earlier, biased or inaccurate data can lead to biased or inaccurate outputs.[18] It's crucial to address these issues to ensure that graph-powered LLMs are used ethically and responsibly.
- Protecting Privacy: Knowledge graphs often contain sensitive information about individuals.[19] It's essential to implement strong privacy protections to prevent misuse and ensure that people's data is used responsibly.
- Addressing Job Displacement: As with any automation technology, there's the potential for job displacement as some tasks currently performed by humans are automated by graph-powered LLMs. It's important to proactively address this issue and ensure a just transition for workers.

A Collaborative Future

The development and deployment of graph-powered LLMs require a collaborative effort between researchers, developers, policymakers, and the public.[20] By working together, we can harness the power of this technology to create a more informed, equitable, and prosperous future for all.

The journey ahead is filled with exciting possibilities, and I'm optimistic that graph-powered LLMs will play a pivotal role in shaping a better world.

Conclusion

From understanding the limitations of current LLMs to delving into the intricacies of knowledge graphs and graph retrieval techniques, we've covered a lot of ground. We've seen how this powerful combination can enhance LLM capabilities, enabling them to be more accurate, knowledgeable, and context-aware. And we've explored the diverse applications of this technology, from revolutionizing customer service and healthcare to transforming education and scientific research.

As we conclude this book, it's clear that graph-powered LLMs represent a significant leap forward in the field of AI. They offer a promising path towards creating AI systems that are not just intelligent but also deeply knowledgeable and capable of understanding and interacting with the world in a more meaningful way.

The journey ahead is filled with exciting possibilities. As the technology continues to evolve, we can expect even more innovative and impactful applications to emerge, shaping the future of how we live, work, and interact with information.

However, it's important to acknowledge the challenges that lie ahead. Ensuring data quality, mitigating bias, addressing ethical considerations, and promoting responsible AI development are crucial for realizing the full potential of graph-powered LLMs and ensuring that they are used to benefit society as a whole.

This book is just the beginning of the conversation. It's an invitation to explore, experiment, and contribute to the growing field of graph-powered LLMs. Whether you're a researcher, developer, or simply curious about the future of AI, I encourage you to join the journey and help shape the future of knowledge and intelligence.